It Was God, All Along

The Moment I Realized
I Wasn't Psychic.

Jennifer Thomas

*Dearest Ilana,
I am so grateful we are
sharing our journey! I love
you so much.
God loves you ~
Love,
your forever
friend —
Jennifer Thomas*

ISBN- 978:1533405562
ISBN- 10: 1533405565

Any correspondence to the author can be directed to itwasgodallalong@gmail.com

Cover photo by Pamela Colonna
Author photo by M.S.

For Carrie Anne, Emily, and Megan:
My heart will always belong to all of you.
I love you more.

Mom: Thank you for your love and support.
I'm forever grateful God chose you to be
my Mother. I love you.

To all of the souls I've lost: Rest in Peace...
until we meet again.

Anna: You'll always be an angel in my eyes.

Geneva: Thank you for your love and support,
and your thoughtful guidance. Love you.

Pam and Kim: Thank you for all of your help
and support. I couldn't have
done it without you. Love you both.

It Was God, All Along

The Moment I Realized
I Wasn't Psychic.

Jennifer Thomas

James 1:6 "But when you ask, you must believe and not doubt, because the one who doubts is like a wave of the sea, blown and tossed by the wind."

Chapter 1

Have you ever had that moment, that instant, when you realized that you really weren't that great of a person? You thought you were. You thought you were fairly nice, fairly patient, fairly intelligent . . . this list could go on and on. Have you believed you were good, but then suddenly found yourself down on your knees, all broken into a thousand pieces, crying out to God telling Him how awful you are? Telling Him how sorry you are? Well, I had that moment, and it was painfully ugly. Brutal. It was actually the best day of my entire life.

Just a month after I turned fifty, my life exploded into an unimaginable thing all it's own, a place I couldn't have imagined. There I was, on the ground, in a puddle of my own tears. The skin on my bare knees was scraping against the cold cement, with every movement my shaking body made. I couldn't stop crying. Leaning on the metal railing of the patio of our second floor apartment, I was crying up to the stars in the dark sky. Trying to cry as quietly as possible, trying not to wake our neighbors, I was crying to God.

"God, I'm sorry. I'm sorry. I'm so sorry." It just went on and on, I couldn't stop. It's all I could say. I stayed there, unable to move for a while. My cries had quieted, my body now gently heaving and shuttering. I just held a gaze up to the sky, feeling complete defeat. I had nothing left, nothing left to say or feel. A certain peace fell over me.

I sat and thought about my life. Childhood, motherhood, adulthood, high school, things were running through my head, memories I had forgotten about. Certain things would cause more tears, others a bit of anger. My emotions were fighting each other, but I didn't have any energy left to fight them.

Eventually I made my way inside, and I sat, exhausted, flipping through the guide trying to find something to watch on television. I needed some sort of distraction, to save myself. Nothing looked appealing. I kept scrolling, and scrolling, into unknown territory on the guide . . . until I saw the name Joyce Meyer Ministries: Enjoying Everyday Life. I pushed the OK button. There she was. "God loves you," she said.

I teared up, thinking to myself, "No, I've been a horrible person, He won't love me, I'm horrible, I'm not a good Christian, I've been a terrible person." My thoughts were battling everything she was saying. The more I watched, the more I liked her personality, and she had an air about her that I could respect. She seemed real. She had been abused, and look at her, she looked happy. She quoted some things from the Bible, and it began to reach me. I grabbed a pencil and paper and began to write the verses down to look up later. I had only done this a few times before, in the months leading up to this night, with a man I was in a relationship with for the previous four years. These verses were hitting me like nothing I had ever heard before. Something was different this time.

I set the DVR to record her shows, and went to bed. It was almost morning. I had a child that would be waking up soon, and she would need me.

Morning greeted me with swollen eyes, a hungry child, and a wounded spirit. I went through the day getting everything done that was required, with the goal of looking up the Bible verses that I had written down the night before. I needed something to heal my wounds, and I needed something quickly. I flipped through my recently acquired Bible, my first, actually, and found 1 Corinthians 13:4-8. "Love is patient, love is kind. It does not envy, it does not boast, it is not proud. It does not dishonor others, it is not self-seeking, it is not easily angered, it keeps no record of wrongs. Love does not delight in evil but rejoices with the truth. It always protects, always trusts, always hopes, always perseveres. Love never fails."

As I read these words, the guilt washed over and through me immediately. I am horrible! I hadn't realized before how bad I really was. I am the worst person ever, I thought as I read. Not patient, sometimes kind, sometimes envious, I've bragged before, I have dishonored others . . . a lot of others. I have been very angry for a while, and oh boy, do I love a good score card in an argument. I didn't think God could possibly love me at all at this point, look at all the evidence.

I was crying again, back out on the patio crying up to the stars. I needed something. I was a mess. If only I had known all of this before! Why hadn't someone really taught me all of this? My life wouldn't have ended up in such a tangled mess.

To really understand part of my struggle, you would have to know something about my family. I was adopted into a family that had two teen-aged boys, one thirteen, the other fourteen. I was only a few days old when they brought me home. One year later, they adopted another newborn girl, and just like that, we became a family of six. We were a fairly typical, nice middle-class family.

I don't know how other families introduce the

topic of adoption to their adopted children, but my family had a sense of humor about it. I was told the family was shopping at K-Mart one day, and there was a "blue light special" on baby girls. Of course, they said, they ran immediately to the blue light and picked the cutest baby girl. I don't know how long I believed the story, but I do still have a vivid memory of babies sitting in a big bin, with the blue light flashing above.

We moved when I was three, to the house in which my parents owned for the next twenty-five years, situated in a nice, middle-class neighborhood in Houston. Dads went off to work and the moms stayed home, for the most part. We rarely locked our back door because neighbors would use that door to come visit. It was a good time.

My sister and I were given a childhood that people dream about for their children, we grew up in one place, a good place. We went to school with the same people from kindergarten through high school. We played outside, all the time, from morning to night. There were many children to play games of kickball, kick the can, or hide and seek. We would get on our bicycles in the morning and not come home until dark, but we always made it home safely. These were the good old days!

By the time I was five, both of my brothers were off at college, and only came home for occasional visits. They married young, both of them, and by the time I was ten, I was an aunt. A month later, I turned eleven, and another niece was born the next day. I felt the maternal urge very young, I think, because of my nieces. I had always loved dolls and babies, and couldn't get enough. I had a little coloring book that featured a girl with a doll that was alive, and I was jealous because my dolls did not come alive. I absolutely loved these babies, and could not wait to become a mother.

I don't know if it was because I was adopted, but I really don't remember ever feeling confident about myself. I'm not sure what the reason was, but I felt different, very different. I never felt like anything about me was as "right" as other kids. People would make comments about other girls being this, or that, and I would immediately think I wasn't whatever this or that was. I don't really know what it was, but I felt there was something wrong with me. I had parents that loved me, we lived in a nice home, and there were plenty friends to play with. It was for the most part an ideal childhood, except for whatever was "wrong" with me.

Most of our weekends were spent out on the land my parents owned, which was about two hours west of Houston. We would generally leave after my dad got home from work on Friday evening, and return Sunday evening. For years we only had a "cabin", which was really a small trailer, accompanied by a "rustic" outhouse. Inside the cabin were several sets of bunk beds, a small kitchen, and dining area. It was rough, but clean. The shower was outside, which was actually a large barrel set atop a metal tripod, with a spout on the bottom. It was not exactly fancy, but this was temporary until we could finally build a house with plumbing. The cabin sat in front of a very large pond, which we called the lake. These were some of my favorite memories as a child, exploring and romping around the land.

Growing up in our family, I viewed church as a big, beautiful place for weddings, funerals, and the occasional place I went with a friend if I slept over at their house on a Saturday night. That was about it for us, and church. In our extended family, there were some church goers, a few Christians here and there, and they lived across town.

When I was little, my friends would ask what

religion we were, and I had to go home and ask. My mother told me I was Methodist, because she was pretty sure I was born in a Methodist Hospital. She was Lutheran, and my father was Baptist. Okay, that sounded good enough, so I was a Methodist. I had no idea what this even meant!

Once when I was seven or eight years old, our family had planned to go to church on Easter Sunday. This was the first time I had ever heard of this in our house, that I could remember. We picked our clothes out the night before . . . this was a really big deal. The next morning, was Easter. I woke up and realized I felt funny. I looked in the mirror, and could plainly see that one side of my face was completely swollen. I went immediately to show my mother. She took one look at me and quickly said, "Well, Jen's got the mumps, we can't go to church." There it was. I ruined our one chance.

When I was fourteen or fifteen, I was invited to a Young Life meeting by a friend. I wasn't sure what to expect, but I knew a couple of people who attended the meetings, and it sounded fun. The night I went, they were discussing an upcoming trip to Colorado, to a camp called Frontier Ranch. It sounded wonderful. They showed us pictures of horseback riding, rappelling, people in costume for skits, just the regular camp stuff.

I had been to a summer camp only one time before, and wasn't sure if I really enjoyed the experience or not, I could never feel completely comfortable in my own skin. The highlight of my first camping experience was a boy I had met. He kissed me behind the archery target, which was actually a large bale of hay. This Young Life camp would be much more intense. Colorado looked beautiful, and the trip sounded exciting, and I think I got a little lost in the sales pitch. I went home that night, and found myself asking my parents if I could go on the trip, still uncertain if I even wanted to go. They thought it was a great opportunity for me, and it was decided. Paperwork was completed, and the money was paid. It was done. Inside I was still unsure and a little afraid, remembering my first camping experience, and how uncomfortable I had felt.

A couple of weeks later, the realization set in while sitting on a bus in the middle of the night, heading to Colorado! There was no turning back. I knew a handful of people on the bus, but I couldn't quite feel at ease, ever. My clothes were wrong, my hair was wrong, my face was wrong. I was just wrong. Not only did I lack self-confidence, I had no knowledge of anything having to do with Young Life, church, the Bible, nothing. I was actually terrified someone would ask me a question about something "religious", and I had nothing. I was Methodist, and had no idea what that meant. That was it. I had nothing. What am I doing?

Why am I on this bus?

Chapter 2

After twenty-something hours on the big gray bus, we finally arrived at Frontier Ranch, just west of Colorado Springs. Now, most of this trip is pretty much a big blur of awkwardness for me, but I have three clear, distinct memories from camp. I believe it was on the first night, or at the first gathering, that we were all sitting around a huge room all focused on our "leaders." They told stories, talked to us about God, played music, and talked about how important it was to actually ask Jesus Christ to come into your heart. They asked everyone to stand up if they had not done so, and wanted to ask Him right then, in front of everyone.

I do not know what got into me, I think I felt some kind of pressure, but there I was, standing up in front of the whole crowd. Me! Me of all people . . . the girl who had nothing, nothing like all of these other kids had. I didn't have any confidence, and no church experience. I said it out loud when it was my turn. "I'm Jennifer, and I'm asking Jesus Christ to come into my heart." I did it. I had no idea what I had just done. No idea. Not a clue.

I was trembling a little, very unsure of myself, and simply sat down in my seat and listened to everyone asking Jesus into their lives. Still, I had no idea what I had just done.

The second memory I have from camp is one of

my greatest accomplishments of my life, overcoming my fear of heights. We were all going rappelling from a cliff. They led us up a path to the top of a rock cliff, strapped us to a rope, and made us walk right off the side. In my mind, I remember it being hundreds of feet tall, but probably in reality, it was most likely somewhere in the neighborhood of forty or fifty feet, just guessing.

The first step was the most terrifying, but once we stepped off they assured us it would be the most exhilarating experience of our lives. For some it was a piece of cake, and the rest of us struggled. I wouldn't even jump off of a high diving board on a dare, or without a dare, no, my fear of heights was real. I felt pressured to do it, so there I was, taking that first step. Holding on to the rope with every ounce of strength within me, I did it.

Slowly, but surely, I made my way all the way down. I'm sure it wasn't graceful, or what you see climbers doing, bouncing off the wall, but I made it all the way down. It truly was exhilarating, and the feeling of accomplishment was something I was not accustomed to feeling, I was never really in situations like this. I remember feeling proud while standing at the bottom, looking up to the top, where I had been standing just a few moments earlier. I did it.

I carried this new found feeling of pride into the next memory from camp, where I would have to face yet another fear, horseback riding. Now, you would think a girl that actually had a horse of her own would not be afraid of horses. Think again.

My father built a barn out on our ranch, with a small corral, and decided his girls should have horses. The day we went to choose a horse, my little sister picked a tall, beautiful Arabian horse named Sheba. I went another way, choosing a small, Shetland pony, named Honey.

How scary could a little pony named Honey be, I ask you?

You'd be surprised. I fell off of that little horse several times, and was even dragged through bull nettle on one occasion. If you've never experienced bull nettle, it's a plant that grows wild, and has little hairs on it. The little hairs inflict an enormous amount of pain into your skin if you touch it.

Now here we were at camp, going horseback riding, and everyone around me was just as excited as they could possibly be. We had our jeans and tennis shoes on for the event, and the fear had already been building up inside of me since breakfast. We made the walk to the stables, a group of at least forty campers, to the best of my recollection. We were all told to pick a horse as they stood in rows, tied to posts, all decked out in their leather saddles.

I quickly searched for a small horse, but people were grabbing their horses so fast, there was no time. I saw a large, pretty brown horse in front of me, and walked up next to it. It seemed gentle, calm, and I was hoping she would stay that way! I was trying my best not to be afraid. I had always heard that horses smell fear, and my track record was not good. We were instructed to let one of the leaders assist us as we mounted our horse. I waited my turn, with anxiousness stirring inside of me. My turn finally came and I put my left foot into the stirrup and swung my right leg up and over. The young man untied my horse, handed the rope to me and told me to walk my horse over and get in the line. I did what I was told. So far, so good.

The line began to move, and we were on our way. As we walked through the beautiful trees along a narrow path, single-file, I began to feel more relaxed, but only a little. This wasn't so bad. My horse, I hoped, knew to follow the horse in front of us, and I wouldn't have to do anything but sit on the saddle and pretend to have fun. I was trying to relax and enjoy the ride, and enjoy the scenery. The girl in front of me was so comfortable on her horse she actually leaned way back and laid down on the horses rear-end, and let go of the reins. I kept thinking her horse would take off running and she would fall off, or the horse would jump and she would fall. I couldn't believe she had that much trust in the horse to let go of the reins. I still, to this day, can remember the envy I felt over her complete lack of fear. I wanted so badly to not be afraid of riding the horse. I wanted to be that girl.

We walked further on the path, and it began to turn into a cliff, and we were literally walking on an edge of a mountain. It was a really narrow switchback. I became more and more anxious when I looked down below, hoping my horse was smart enough not to fall off. I could see the end coming, and finally we walked into a beautiful meadow. It was flat, with trees all around the edges, and our line began to form an "L" shape as we walked around the meadow.

Without any warning, my horse suddenly jumped. I screamed. She bolted quickly out into the center of the meadow, and began to buck. It happened so quickly, I was just holding on with everything I had. I only weighed about a hundred pounds, so my chances weren't very good. After the fourth or fifth buck, I went flying in the air, landing hard on the ground, on my side. I was trying to figure out where my horse was, I just knew it would step on me. I couldn't see. I could taste dirt. I was stunned. I began to feel some pain in my arm, and my hip. I was lying there, somewhat paralyzed, in shock. After a few moments, I realized what had happened and also realized that everyone was looking at me. I was mortified.

One of the leaders quickly came to help me up, and was walking me over to his own horse.

As we walked he was asking me if I was alright, and I felt something strange in the seat of my pants. There was an enormous hole in the seat of my pants, they had split wide open. I knew everyone could now see my underwear, and this made my eyes tear up. I was so humiliated. He took his shirt off, helped me tie it around my waist, quickly, and helped me onto his horse. I rode behind him, sitting just behind his saddle, for the rest of the ride. My eyes were filled with tears, I couldn't see, and I kept my head down on his back the entire ride.

My arm was throbbing, my hip hurt, but my pride was wounded beyond measure. I could hear giggles and laughs from behind us, and I knew I was a joke. Why did I choose that horse? Why me? Did it sense my fear? What in the world is wrong with me? I wanted to go home.

When we got back to the camp, he took me straight to the nurse. They were relieved there was nothing broken, I don't think they knew I felt like my whole existence was broken.

That is probably the last thing I remember about that whole trip, and it was pretty much the end of my Young Life days. I don't remember ever going to another meeting after we returned home, I simply couldn't shake the humiliation I had felt at camp. Ever.

Chapter 3

My life began to stray from the traditional over the next few years, about the time I was to enter my senior year of high school. I was on the younger side of most people in my grade. I started kindergarten at four, and turned five over a month later. Going into my senior year of high school, I was only sixteen. My sister had been a little rebellious as a teen. She and my mother had been going round and round for a while, battling through all the normal things parents with rebellious teens go through. After exhausting some other options, my father sat me down in the dining room one day to talk, with tears in his eyes. I had only seen my father cry at his father's funeral, when I was about twelve, and when his barn full of ranch equipment burned to the ground. This was different.

He explained that my mother and my sister couldn't work through their issues, which were causing conflict in my parent's marriage. To save the family, and save them from divorce, they needed me to move into an apartment with my sister. She was only fifteen at the time, and by the time we moved into the apartment, I was barely seventeen.

I admit it was a tad exciting at first, but soon the realization set in, it was only a little one bedroom apartment. It was located just around the corner from our neighborhood. The second realization I experienced was the fact that this would have been wonderful, if my sister and I had been close, but we fought. We fought to the death, mostly. We always knew how to push each others buttons in an instant.

There we were, moving into our own place. Two little girls, basically, without supervision. I really had no idea what to expect. I certainly didn't expect what I got. Our friends suddenly had their own "getaway," a place they could come and go as they pleased. The parties were never-ending, the late nights exhausting. Needless to say, my grades were already slipping beyond recognition. I really wanted to go home. Something inside of me wanted to please my father, be a hero in his eyes, and I did not want to let him down. I was, after all, "saving the family."

My sister and I had already experienced our share of freedom, even before the apartment. Most weekends our parents would drive out to their land which we called "the ranch." All of our friends knew they were gone almost every weekend, and we had quite a few parties. There was alcohol and smoking. It was all bad.

It was so well-known that they were usually gone, in fact, that late one night some of our friends, all boys, came over looking for everyone. They saw my car out front, but were actually looking for my sister and her friends. They knocked on the door, and nobody answered. They saw light coming from the back of the house, so they walked around to the back to see who was there. We did not have a fence, so you could walk around the house easily. They looked in the windows of our den, and saw me lying on the floor, asleep in front of the television. The boys started knocking on the windows. I didn't move. They knocked harder and harder. Finally they ran around banging on different doors, windows, and rang the doorbell. Nothing. I didn't move, and didn't wake up.

That night my mother was actually at home, trying

to sleep upstairs, and suddenly hears all of the noise coming from downstairs. She got up, grabbed her gun, walked down the stairs, and opened the front door. She shot a few times up in the air, and the boys went running. She went back to bed, and I still laid there, fast asleep on the floor. I never heard any of it.

I went to school Monday morning, only to hear the tall tale of how my mother had tried to "kill" the boys, and how they heard bullets whizzing by their heads. It was hilarious, because I knew she had only shot in the air to scare them off. From that day, the late-night visitors and parties became fewer, and fewer, until we moved to the apartment.

Living in an apartment now, this was an entirely new kind of freedom. Absolutely no parental guidance whatsoever. After a few months of this apartment living, I drove home from school one day, got out of my car, and was walking to the sidewalk that led into the courtyard. I noticed a figure standing in a long window. It caught my eye, and when I looked closer, I noticed it was a man, fully nude. He was standing naked, watching me walk towards him. I quickly looked down, and kept walking as fast as I could to my door. I went in as quickly as possible, trembling, and didn't really know what I was supposed to do. I did nothing. I told a couple of my friends, but did nothing. From that day forward, I parked a little further down in the parking lot, and walked around the other side of the building.

Most of our neighbors we had met were really sweet to all of us, even though we were so young, and most likely loud. One of our neighbors would leave his windows open and we could hear him playing his piano and singing. He played in various places around town, but we were able to enjoy it while sitting outside around the pool. Another neighbor was a boy who went to our high school, and lived there with his mother. We became friends with him quickly after we moved in.

The man across the hall from us was a friendly, handsome man, maybe in his early thirties. He left his door open quite frequently and would always say hello when we came and went. One day when I was getting home from school he was standing in his doorway, with a glass of wine in hand. It seemed like he was waiting for me. He told me he had been injured at work, and had to come home early, and was hoping to see me. He said he could use some company, and even offered me a glass of wine. I was only seventeen. The attention felt nice, and my thought process was that he was treating me more like a grown woman, instead of a young girl. I felt compelled to act like the grown-up he thought I was, and without hesitation, I walked into his apartment. I didn't want to be rude. I took the glass of red wine, and sipped it while pretending to like it. I drank it all.

The next thing I remember was waking up and feeling groggy. I was on his bed. My body felt strange, and I was hurting in certain areas, some very private areas. I got up and walked into the living room, where he was sitting and watching television. I was trying so hard to figure out what was happening, but before I could really say anything, he told me he had to leave. I grabbed my things and walked across the hall to my apartment. I locked the door. It was quiet. There was nobody there. I felt so strange, so confused, and my body hurt.

I was trying to put the pieces together, and the mental image of him naked popped into my head. It was finally dawning on me what had happened. I began to feel afraid, and more confused. I was having a really hard time waking up, but it was all starting to make sense. I felt dirty.

I needed to take a bath, quickly. I will wash it away. What would people think of me now? They will say I did something to flirt, or make him think I wanted this. I was so, so ashamed. So embarrassed. I told no one.

I undressed and put my robe on, and just as I was walking into the bathroom to run a bath, I heard a knock at the door. My body froze. I thought it was him. I was mortified, thinking he was back again. I crept quietly to the door to look out the peephole, and to my relief, it was two of our guy friends. They would protect me now, from him. I opened the door quickly, and let them in. They weren't in my close group of friends, but I knew them pretty well.

I told them to sit and watch television while I took a bath, and then we could hang out. I'm thinking the whole time that they are my protection. They began to ask me if I had anything on underneath my robe.

My mind still a little foggy, I couldn't understand why they were asking me this. I quickly said, "Y'all, stop, please, I need to take a bath real quick. Just watch T.V."

They began to pull on my robe, the belt, trying to untie it. I kept telling them to stop. I was walking backwards trying to get away from them, but they just would not stop. The next thing I knew they had walked me backwards right onto my bed, and were touching me all over. Still not feeling completely awake, still sort of in a daze, I had no real strength. I was trying to fight them off, telling them to stop, but they were laughing and continuing to touch me. They kept laughing. They would hold me down and suck on my neck to leave marks, "hickeys" for everyone to see.

They thought it was funny, and I was fighting as hard as I could to get them to stop. They had no idea what

I had already been through just hours before. I needed help.

They finally stopped, and when they did, still thinking it was funny, and now even making fun of me, they left.

I ran a bath and cried and cried. I felt so completely ashamed of myself. I knew I was completely worthless, and now I had red and purple marks all over my neck to prove it.

Going to school the next day was probably one of the low points of my high school years. I tried to cover my neck with makeup and clothing, but there was no way to completely hide the marks. All day long my friends, and others, would ask me who gave me all of the hickeys on my neck. I tried to say it was just someone I was dating, or that it was just a joke, but I knew they would know I was lying. I was so ashamed, felt so dirty, and a little angry. I did nothing. I felt so helpless, so powerless, and so worthless. I wanted out of high school. I wanted to go home. There were no options.

My self-worth had plummeted to an even lower low, if possible, when I realized my grades in two of my classes were dipping to a failing grade. I was scared. Every day was like living in a dazed state, going through motions, I was terrified. I couldn't function.

I was sitting in my English class one day, and I heard one of the "smart" girls ask our teacher out loud, "Is anyone failing and not going to be graduating with us?" I froze. I looked up at my teacher, just in time to see her nodding her head up and down, whispering my name and pointing right at me! I couldn't believe it. How could she? I felt the tears pooling up in my eyes, as I looked down at my desk, not knowing what to do.

I gathered my things and walked right out of her

class. I ran down the ramp outside and straight to my car, and drove "home" to the apartment as fast as I could. I was sobbing the entire way. Everything was wrong. How in the world would I tell my parents I wasn't going to graduate? A whole new set of problems to face, alone.

I never went back to my English class. Frankly, I stopped going to my Government class, as well. I knew my grades were failing in that class, too, and thought I'd save myself more humiliation and just stop going.

I was not feeling good about myself at this point in my life, nothing about me was good. I had no direction, no guidance, no protection, I was just lost. Completely lost.

Chapter 4

The end of my senior year finally came, and to no one's surprise, I did not graduate with all of my friends. There was a part of me that was ashamed of myself, because I knew I could have made the grades if I had really tried. Another part of me was relieved that I was out of that school, which had become a place of torture. I felt a bit of real freedom for the first time, a freedom I never felt even living outside of my parents home. This was more of an escape than having my own apartment had ever been. I quickly signed up for summer school to earn the credits for the classes I needed in order to get my diploma. I was determined to graduate high school, even if it was a little later than everyone else.

The high school hosting the summer school was about thirty minutes away, and it would last for several weeks. My morning routine was the same every day, get ready, grab two pieces of toast and a coke for the drive. My first class was Government, and English second. School started at eight o'clock, and I was surprisingly early the first couple of days. I was determined to get that diploma. Some of my friends had started summer jobs, which made it easier for me to deal with still having to go to school, for the most part. We would all hang out in the evenings, but the nights weren't lasting too late to interfere with their jobs, or my school.

It was working out, until the Friday of the first week of summer school. Everyone was going to the beach.

I couldn't resist. One absence wouldn't hurt, I had two more just in case. The next Monday came and I had not felt very well, most likely from all of the weekend activities. I slept through my alarm, and missed my first class. There wasn't enough time to get ready and get to my second class, it would be too late. Second absence, after only one week. I already had two absences. I could do it. I could still do it.

For the rest of the week I tried to get back on my schedule. I was completing all of the work and it did not seem as hard the second time around, I was actually doing very well. Two weeks completed. I felt a sense of something resembling pride, even though it wasn't much of an accomplishment. This was what I should have done the first time around, but at least now, it was something. Monday of the third week, I got to my second class, English, and tried to think of something to write in my journal, the assignment every day for the first ten minutes of class. I couldn't think of anything, and I just sat staring out the window. I started to daydream. Then, it got a little weird. I was daydreaming about sitting in my seat, in that class, and hearing a knock on the door. The teacher would walk over to the door as it opened, and there would be the security officer, in her uniform. She would say "I need Jennifer to grab her things and come with me."

I would actually see myself gathering my things, walking to the door, and following the security woman down the hall and down the stairs, through the courtyard and to the office. As we would approach the office, I would peer into the window of the principal's office, and immediately see my mother sitting in a chair, crying. That's where it ended, every time. I had that same daydream every day that week, multiple times a day. The dream was so long and detailed, and I had never experienced anything like this, it was bizarre. I just knew there was something wrong with me. I wrote it all down in my journal, "There is something wrong with me." I couldn't understand what was happening, why I was doing this every day. I was awake, but having this weird dream, unable to stop. I wanted to stop, but I didn't know how. I couldn't control this "daydream," or whatever it was.

Friday came, and once again I found myself in a place other than school. I was home, because I didn't feel like going to school. Third absence. There were no more absences to use. I would have to attend every single day until the last if I wanted my diploma. I was pretty angry at myself, but that was nothing unusual. I could do it. I could still do it.

That night, my friends were all coming over to hang out by the pool at my apartment. The piano player was having a party that night, and we could hear his music as we sat around the pool below. It was a good night, until it got really late, and everyone became intoxicated. An argument broke out in our group. Two of the guys were beginning to argue, and then it escalated to yelling. The rest of us couldn't figure out what the issue was, but there was something big going on. One of them, Mark, told me it was because of me, in part. I asked what I did. The other one told me he had feelings for me, but he knew I had a crush on Mark, and he couldn't control his emotions. He was very upset, and Mark was trying to calm him down. The alcohol was not helping the situation, at all.

Mark was one of my best friends. I had known him since junior high, but had developed a friendship in high school. He was an only child, and I was close with his mother, as well. I had introduced my good friend Maggie to Mark at a football game the year before, and they had been in an on-again, off-again relationship ever since. I had a crush on him, but never interfered in their relationship. They were both my friends. At this point they were no longer together, and I had become even closer with Mark, and his mother, even going on a little vacation with them, but we had remained good friends.

When the fight escalated, I asked them both to leave, out of fear I would get in trouble for the noise. They both became angry at me, and left. The party was over, and a few people helped me clean up after everyone, and soon they all left.

The next morning, Saturday, I went over to my parents house and hung out there most of the day. I helped with a little yard work, it had always been my job to sweep after my dad mowed the yard. I didn't live there anymore, but still spent time at "home." A friend came over and we watched television, nothing special. Sunday, I went with my parents across town to see my grandmother, aunt and uncle. We spent the day with them, something that was really important to my father, spending time with his family. My dad couldn't sit still, ever, and we went visiting a lot. After a long day, I went home to the apartment, to get prepared for school the next morning. I had to be there every day from now on, no excuses, no skipping. I could do it.

Monday morning, same as every other day, two pieces of toast and a coke and I was out the door, on time. I arrived at school a few minutes early, and went to class. I sat at my desk and looked up at the chalkboard to see what the assignments were, and began to write it all down. The bell rang and the teacher began to tell us the agenda for the day, and suddenly I began to feel really strange. A sweat broke out all over my face, and my mouth began to water. I knew I was going to be physically ill. As she was still talking, I grabbed my purse and literally ran right in front of her and out the door. I ran as quickly as I could to the restroom. I became very ill.

I splashed some water on my face, rinsed my mouth, and walked outside. I sat down at the top of the stairs, to feel the fresh air on my face. A few minutes later I heard footsteps behind me, it was my teacher. She sat down next to me. "Are you okay?" she asked.

I explained to her what had happened, and that I didn't know why, I had felt fine that morning. Looking back now, I'm sure she guessed I was pregnant, but no, I wasn't. I rarely became ill, and for some reason this time it felt really strange. She told me to get some fresh air and come back to class when I felt better, and I did. It was bothering me, but I was focused on getting my work completed.

English class started, and I wrote in my journal about everything I had done over the weekend. We began our work for the day, doing research for our papers, and I was reading when I heard it . . . the knock at the door.

I paused for a second, and then looked up to see my teacher walking to the door, as it opened. I saw the security officer poke her head inside the classroom, and heard her say my name. I heard her say I needed to gather my things and get to the office.

You know that feeling you get, when you get little chills all over your body, and you don't want to move? This is what I was feeling. By the time my teacher turned around and told me to gather my things, I was already doing it, I knew what was happening, but I didn't really know *what* was happening. I was scared. As I walked to the door I felt like everyone was staring at me. I became so aware of every little noise, every little thing going on around me.

I followed her down the hall, and when we got to the top of the stairs, I asked her what was going on. She simply said "everything will be okay," in a calm voice. I walked behind her all the way down the stairs, and across the courtyard, towards the principal's office. The window, I could see the window. As I walked by, I slowly peered in the window . . . and there she was. My mother, sitting in the chair across from his desk, crying.

When we walked into the office, the security officer pointed ahead to the principals door, and motioned for me to go inside. I did, slowly, and turned to my right to look at my mom. I had never seen her cry like this in my life. All I said was, "who died?"

"Mark."

All I could say was no. Just no.

Mark was gone. I had to get to his mom's house, and quickly. When we walked to my mom's car, I noticed another friend of mine sitting in the front seat. She had been the one to tell my mom about Mark, and had driven with her to come get me. As we drove, a thousand thoughts were running through my head, and we were all in shock. All I could think about was Mark's mom, he was her only child. He was her whole world. She was good to all of us, his friends, even having us all over for a dinner party recently. She treated us like adults, with such respect, and loved Mark so much, it really showed. Her whole world, was gone.

When we arrived at her house, there were already people there, going in and out of the front door. A man stood in front of a large window, and as we got closer, we could see the glass was broken, and on the ground. My mother asked him what happened, and he explained that Mark's work had called to tell his mother he had died.

They told her over the phone, which she threw through the window. How horrible. Over the phone.

As we walked through the front door we saw several people walking around. There was someone on the phone talking in a low voice. It was quiet. We quickly asked someone where she was and they pointed to the living room, in the back of the house. There she was, lying on the sofa.

I immediately walked to her and bent down to hug her. She raised up a bit, and hugged me, and said "Hi Shug," (short for sugar) in her classy southern style, "he went by your apartment yesterday to apologize to you, but said you weren't home. He said y'all were in a fight."

We were in a fight. And now he's gone. I would never get to make up with him. He's gone.

He was her only child. He was only seventeen.

No. Just No.

This tragedy, and the daydreams I had leading up to that day changed the way I thought. Every time I had a bad thought, or "saw something" in my thoughts about someone dying, I would question it. I would think "is this really going to happen, or am I making myself think these things," it never ever ended. It was constant. It was scary. I lived in fear of my thoughts for years to come.

I had no doubt the reason I had been ill, and the timing of my sudden sickness, was all related to Mark's death. He had the accident just minutes after arriving at work that morning, around eight o'clock. The timing was too close for it to be anything else. Any time I felt the slightest bit ill after this, I was convinced someone was dying. It was always an instant thought. Between my thoughts and this fear whenever I would feel ill at all, I felt so changed after Mark's death. My perspective of life also changed drastically, seeing a mother lose her only child. I couldn't imagine anything more painful, or tragic. It was so unfair.

I began to realize just how fragile life is, and saw a glimpse at how dark and painful it could be. Seeing a mother suffer in this way never left me. It was something I thought about frequently, because I knew I wanted nothing more than to be a mother myself. There was now a bit of a frightening side to motherhood.

Chapter 5

The funeral was on a beautiful, sunny day, in a small town where Mark's mom had grown up. It was such a sad time in my life, in all of our lives. This event was the beginning of an internal struggle I fought for a very long time. The usual steps of grief from losing our friend Mark were challenging for all of us, and in some ways it made our friendships in our group even closer. I was trying to deal with the grief, and the sorrow I had for Mark's mother. I was also trying to figure out why I had that experience of the "daydream." The daydream that had come true.

The daydream coupled with getting physically ill confirmed to me, that at the very least, somehow I knew it was going to happen. I tried to talk about it with a few people, but they would compare it to something they had experienced that somehow seemed to trivialize it. It didn't help, and I remained confused, questioning everything. Losing a set of keys, and then having a "vision" of finding them in a drawer was not quite the same experience I had just been through. One friend told me I was psychic. Psychic? Was that it? It made sense, psychics see the future, right? Another friend said I was clairvoyant. Interesting. It was always in the back of my mind, just nagging at me. People weren't understanding what I was saying, and I felt so much judgment, I stopped talking about it.

Maggie and I became closer and closer after Mark

passed away, and often went together to check on his mom. The first Easter after his death, we made an Easter basket for her, because it was something Mark had done in the past for his mom. One day when we were visiting her, the three of us quietly laid in the dark on her bed. Maggie was on one side of her, I was on the other, and she held our hands. We talked quietly for a long time. She told us about some dreams that either she, or a friend of hers had about Mark. She asked if we ever dreamed of him, and told us that if we did, to write it down and tell her about it.

She told us about the after life, and it was the first time I had really ever heard about it in detail, and I couldn't really wrap my head around it. I wasn't raised talking about God and an after life, but it felt real. It was a struggle for me, and I was still struggling with the daydream event. I was still trying to deal with all the bad things that had happened to me. It was all piling on, and I still had no direction, and no guidance. I was still lost.

It had been two years now, since Mark's death, and Maggie and I were still close, and hanging out a lot. I had finally earned my diploma, but had to take night school after that awful summer. The summer school would not let me miss another day for Mark's funeral, so I was forced to drop out. That next semester, I was changed, and I finally graduated. I went to work doing clerical work in an office, but Maggie and I spent almost every evening and weekend together. Our bond had become so strong through our grief over Mark.

She had a new boyfriend, and her parents had bought her a horse. I went to the stables a few times with Maggie, and always rode with her, not on my own horse, of course. Her new beau worked at another stables, and had a small little apartment there, where we hung out a few times. We were more like sisters, than friends, we could argue and fight, but could forget about it in a second.

There was a guy that I had a crush on, and he had joined our "group" about this time. We hit it off quickly, and he would flirt with me constantly. I was nineteen now, and did not have any more confidence than I had at seventeen, but I was still trying. He was the cutest guy I had ever met, and I loved it when people told me we looked alike, and would make a great couple.

I have to tell you, when you are adopted and people tell you that you look like someone, there is always that possibility in the back of your mind that you are related to that person. Every time someone said he and I looked alike, this little thought crossed my mind. I knew the chances were slim, but I did think about it sometimes.

Months of flirting, hanging out, going to the dollar movie theater and watching three movies in one day, we did all kinds of fun things. We spent a lot of time together. He never made the "move" on me, so I began to worry.

My friends either said something was wrong, or that he was just a nice guy. I wanted things to progress in our relationship, I wanted to be his girlfriend. One night when we were all playing pool together at a neighborhood pool hall, he showed up. Maggie and several friends in our group were there, as well. It was going great, we were having fun, until I noticed Maggie talking to him. My guy. It made me nervous. He still flirted with me, but she kept talking to him. She knew I liked him. I was getting upset. He left, a few others left, and Maggie and I were soon driving back to her house, where I had left my car. When we got in the car, she told me she liked him. My guy. She wanted to go out with him.

This became an argument, and within the ten

minutes it took to drive to her house, it became a fight.

We were saying horrible things to each other, and yelling in the car, which spilled out onto her front lawn. We were literally on the ground pulling hair, slapping, and yelling, when the lights came on. Her front porch lights were shining directly on us. We heard the front door open, and we both stood up quickly. I ran to my car and drove home, to my parents home. I was living at home again, since my sister had moved in with her boyfriend. It was only a couple of blocks away, so I got home in a couple of minutes. Crying, my skin burning on my face from slaps, and my head hurting from having my hair pulled. I know she was in the same shape from my slaps and pulls.

It was quite embarrassing. I couldn't believe we had just fought like that, but I was so angry at what she was doing, and would surely accomplish. She had everything boys loved, the figure, the free spirit, and then there was me. Awkward, horrible, worthless me.

A week or so after that night, I was to meet friends at the restaurant where Maggie worked. I had worked there also, as had a handful of our friends. The manager of the restaurant was our friend, and she would hire us as servers, or hostesses. It was a great, neighborhood type restaurant, full of the same regulars, daily.

I arrived at the restaurant, saw my friends at the bar, and joined them. We were to meet there, and then go to a couple of different parties. After a little while, it was time to go, and I stood up to leave, and I saw her. Maggie, standing down at the end of the bar. She was working. I noticed she had this pink glow all around her, from the lamp behind her. I smiled, she smiled back. I missed her. I thought about walking down there, to apologize for our fight, but everyone was ready to leave, and I didn't have time. I waved and smiled again, and she waved and smiled back at me. We were good, I thought, I'll apologize tomorrow. We'll make up, tomorrow.

That night after the parties I went home to my parents house, and went to sleep. The next morning I heard the phone ring, but tried to go back to sleep. A few minutes later I heard my mom call my name.

I walked out of my room and down the hall to her bedroom. She was sitting on her bed, coffee cup in hand. I laid down on the bed, on my dad's side.

"That was one of your friends, I've got some bad news," she said. "Maggie was on her way home from a party late last night and was hit by a drunk driver," she said. "She's gone," she said.

What? No. That can't be true.

No. Just no.

This cannot, cannot be happening, again.

I went numb, and stayed numb for days. I went into some kind of daze. I couldn't believe this had happened to Maggie. She was gone. I cried, but I was just numb. The sadness, the guilt, the confusion, I was going through so many emotions after that, I had a really hard time finding something to grasp, something to hold on to. I felt like I was just floating around, bouncing around, and nothing felt right. I was even more lost than I had ever been before.

She was buried next to Mark, and it was surreal going through another funeral, almost the exact funeral, two years later. It was the same everything. I don't really remember much from that day, I just remember going. It was too much. I'm not sure I dealt with her loss, I don't think I wanted to accept another death. There was so much guilt over our fight, the guilt and shame blocked any healing, the healing I needed so desperately.

When Maggie died so tragically, so soon after Mark, my whole existence became extremely fragile. I began to change in ways I didn't really even notice until later in life. I did realize one change, adding to my fear of life, I now had a fear of death. I was terrified of death. I became afraid of things suddenly, things that could injure or kill me. I began to wear my seat belt every time I got into the car, before it was even a law. I stopped taking little risks, any activity that was the slightest bit dangerous. It was a real fear.

One day, while at work, I decided to take my lunch hour and go home to eat. I thought my mom would be there, and I would grab a bite to eat and visit with her. I got there and the house was empty, so I looked in the pantry and found a snack. I grabbed a pack of peanut butter crackers and a drink, and left. I was driving back to work, eating the crackers. When I looked down into the pack I saw something moving in the peanut butter part, in between the crackers. I quickly noticed they were little worm-like things. I had already eaten four of these, and began to panic. I looked up and saw an Emergency Clinic up ahead, and exited the freeway as fast as I could. I drove up, parked, and ran inside the clinic. I told the woman at the front desk I needed help! I showed her the crackers with these weird little worms wiggling around in them, and told her I had eaten some of them.

She told me to wait a moment, and would have a doctor come to the front. As I stood there waiting, in my skirt, blouse, pantyhose and heels, and my big 80's hair, I suddenly noticed there were a lot of people looking at me. I looked around at all the people waiting their turn, and thought if only they knew how sick I was about to become, they would understand my urgency. I was hoping I wasn't going to die right there in front of these unsuspecting, innocent people. The doctor walked up to me, put his hand on my shoulder, and calmly explained that I had just eaten a little dose of protein, and that most likely nothing would happen.

What? Nothing? This is nothing?

I felt so incredibly stupid. I was nineteen, and clearly not operating on logic. When I told my mom later that day, she said I probably gave the doctor a good story to tell on the golf course. Okay, so I was a bit dramatic, but the fear was real!

Shortly after Maggie's death, I was working back at the restaurant, with the guy I had the crush on, and a couple of other friends. It was difficult, to say the least, to feel "normal" again, and get back to life. I had lost another best friend. I was such a lost person, still trying to find something to hold on to, or someone. There was a man that frequented the restaurant, and seemed to have many friends there. His office was close by, and several of his colleague's would stop in after work for the happy hour. The happy hour food was free, and delicious.

He had asked me out on a date recently, and I had gone out with him. The guy I liked still seemed a little distant, and I began to lose hope in him. He would see me talking to the man at the bar and tease me, but would never tell me if he had feelings for me, or make a move. I grew impatient, and the first time the man asked me out, I went. He was older, handsome, a businessman.

He was the first man to ever take me to a nice restaurant, or on a real date. He drove a flashy sports car, and loved to show it off, to anyone and everyone. He seemed to really like me, and I began to have feelings for him. One night, I was at home, and the guy I had thought I was so in love with, the one that wouldn't make a move, showed up at my front door. He asked me to go driving with him, and I went. We drove to a little nearby lake. He told me he had taken me for granted, and wanted a chance.

I had wanted him to say these things for so long, but somehow it didn't seem right at this point. I was already looking ahead to being more settled down. I needed to settle down. My new man talked of the future, and it sounded like security to me, something I think I was desperate for. It wasn't a conscious thing at all, but it was a real need.

Sitting out by a small lake, under the stars, I finally heard the words I had longed to hear, but they were too late. That was the end of the old crush, the end of any possibility of a relationship with him. I was already invested in my new relationship.

I needed to feel secure, more than anything, I believe. I continued to date the older man, and we were married two years later, when I was only twenty-one. I found something to hold on to, and I was holding on tight. I wanted to be a wife, a mother, and I wanted it fast. I craved motherhood. I had failed at so many other things, but had wanted to be a mother since I was very young. It's really all I ever wanted to be, a mother.

By the time I was thirteen, I had two nieces, and two nephews, and I spent as much time as I could with them. When I was old enough to drive, I took them everywhere I went, took them to movies, bowling, the park. I enjoyed being their aunt very much. Now I wanted my own.

After a year of trying, and no results, a neighbor suggested I make an appointment with her boss, one of the top fertility doctors in Houston. She made an appointment for me and very soon after, I was in surgery having the problem corrected. Shorty after surgery, while on a mild fertility medicine, I was pregnant. I lost it within six weeks, but quickly became pregnant again. This time I gave birth to a beautiful baby girl. I was almost twenty-four. She was my world. For the first time in my life I felt unconditional love, for my precious baby girl.

Our marriage wasn't the greatest, there were problems. He got a "promotion" that led him to Florida four to five days a week, and it was a little too much freedom for him. I decided I needed some type of college degree, because I would most likely end up a single mother at some point. I enrolled in school, and couldn't believe I found myself sitting in a classroom again after swearing it off forever.

A few months into my classes, I was getting a divorce, going to school, and raising a toddler on my own. It was difficult, but I had found a new sense of pride in not only being a mother, but also being a student, after failing so miserably in high school. When my English/Literature instructor handed one of my papers back to me one day, it had a big, red "A" on it, with the words, "great job," and "flashes of brilliance!" I cried. I knew I could do it, all that time, I knew I could have done better in high school. This simple grade, on a random paper, had just given me something really precious that I had lost years before.

Shortly after my divorce, I was hanging around two old friends from high school, whenever my daughter was with her dad for his visitation. We would go out to different bars, restaurants, and meet up in a group. One of them was dating a guy, and one of his friends came along. They all knew the friend pretty well, I thought. He began to call me. We would talk for hours on the phone, and see each other in the group.

He seemed to be nice, and I thought I could trust

him because they knew him, and would tell me if there was anything weird about him. We began to date. He would give me flowers and bring gifts for my daughter, and seemed to genuinely care for us. By the time I graduated, (both on time and with a GPA I could be proud of) I had been dating him for over a year and had known him for two. We decided to get married at a Justice of the Peace, when my daughter was almost four years old. Although there was some conflict between my mother and me over the marriage, I felt things were going well again. Finally.

Chapter 6

The day we were married I told my new husband, Ron, that since we wanted more children, a sibling for my daughter, I thought I should go off of birth control that day. I had such a hard time before, I thought, and even required surgery to get pregnant, it could possibly take years again. He seemed fine with this idea, and I never thought about it again. Two months later, I was pregnant. I was in shock, and couldn't believe how wonderful, it only took two months this time! When I told him the good news, his reaction took me by surprise. He asked me to terminate the pregnancy.

What? Terminate?

I was dumbfounded.

"I thought you wanted a baby, I thought you said you wanted a sibling for my daughter," I kept saying, over and over. "I thought you were a Christian," I said. He had told me a hundred times that he was a Christian, and that he went to a Christian school, and that he was the "big man on campus" at that Christian school. Now he wants me to terminate a pregnancy, when it had been so hard for me to the conceive the daughter I already had.

I had thought I would have to go through another surgery, take more fertility drugs, and I was prepared for another struggle. I could not believe how lucky, to be pregnant after only a couple of months this time. I had always thought I had been fortunate to be adopted, and for this reason alone, I could never terminate a pregnancy. It just wasn't something I could do. There was no way, absolutely no way I was going to do such a thing.

"What do you care, you're an atheist," he said.

What? Atheist? What in the world is he saying to me? I was standing there in total shock. Pregnant.

I was stunned. What had I done? Who is this person?

My hormones kicked into high gear very quickly, and he, I think, probably wanted to end the marriage, as well. I wanted to end the marriage. I was so mortified I had married this person, and especially since my mother wasn't thrilled I was marrying him in the first place. I was too embarrassed to say anything to anyone. I did not want to hear about my gigantic mistake from anyone. I simply had to hold on. Tensions were high, and it was a challenge, but I held on feeling like I had no choice. I had made a mess of my life once again, and probably messed things up for my daughter, and the precious baby growing inside of me.

My daughter and I flew up to Boulder, Colorado to visit my brother and his wife, about the time I was just beginning to show, at about three months. They had lived there for a while, and I absolutely loved the state. I had been there several times, and had always fantasized about living there, but never really thought I would leave Texas.

They took us down to Pearl Street, in Boulder, which was lined with all sorts of shops and restaurants, and plenty of fun things for kids. There were gigantic rocks in the middle of the street, for children to climb all over. There were street performers everywhere, and one clown in particular. As I walked by him, he smiled, and immediately said "you're having a little girl." What? How did he even know I was pregnant? It was the very first day I had worn a maternity top, and I couldn't believe I looked that big already. Well, actually, that's not all true, I get really large while pregnant. I was always hoping that nobody would really notice. I knew the clown had a fifty percent chance of being right, but never really thought about it much after that day.

About two days into this trip, I was ready to move to Colorado. We spent a day in Estes Park, and there was no question in my mind about moving. It was so beautiful, and I felt so good there, I thought it was something in the air. Everywhere we went felt like fresh air. There was a gorgeous view from every direction, no matter where we were. I felt more alive than I had ever felt. The mountains were truly majestic.

I asked Ron if he would consider starting a new life in Colorado. I knew he had spent a good amount of time there, since his parents had owned a vacation home there years before. He said yes, and that there was a business we could start, a business a friend of his had going in a few different cities in Texas. He didn't see why we couldn't start our own business up in Denver. Things were sounding good, moving forward.

By the time I was seven months pregnant, we were loading a moving truck, and heading north. He had gone up a few weeks before and found a small townhouse for us to rent temporarily until we could buy our own home. His friend had told him how to start the business, and we were getting it going as soon as we got there. Things were falling into place, and the pregnancy was going well.

I gave birth early in the morning, on a cold day at the beginning of spring. We came home from the hospital on the third day, with our beautiful baby girl. I felt so lucky, I now had two sweet girls of my own.

My oldest daughter, Rachel, immediately fell madly in love with her new baby sister, Hannah. I was madly in love with her, as well. I was so happy. Motherhood seemed like "home" to me, it was the most important thing I could ever do. Motherhood gave me purpose like nothing I had ever felt.

The day after we got home from the hospital, Hannah was four days old. I was on the second floor of our townhouse, sitting in bed early in the morning breast-feeding her. I heard a knock on the front door, and then a familiar "hello." It was Ron's mother's voice. They had moved to Boulder from Houston, just before the birth of Hannah, and had rented an apartment across the street from our home. As soon as I heard her voice, I heard someone running up the stairs. It was Ron, and he walked quickly into the room, and grabbed Hannah from me. He literally ripped her from my breast, and said "mom wants to see her."

"She's eating!" I snapped back, angered.

He turned, with the baby, and walked down the stairs. It was an important moment in our lives, it was the beginning of a constant battle. Hannah. Our sweet baby girl. I had carried her for over nine months, felt her every little move, falling more and more in love with her with every little kick. The love I felt was overwhelming, the attachment to that sweet little helpless soul grew every minute. Flooded with hormones, I was fighting for my rights as her mother, to do what was best for her, fighting against my own husband, her father.

As I sat there on the bed, crying, angry, I was sure Ron's mother had probably had *her* breakfast, and would want her four-day-old granddaughter to have hers!

I tried my best to get through the next few months, which were filled with power struggles, and fights for control. He would decide to take Hannah to dinner with his parents, and when she was only a couple of months old. I would say no. He wouldn't care, we would fight, and he would walk out the door with her in her little car seat. It was challenging, to say the least. My maternal instincts were constantly overruled, and our little family was always under stress.

Our business was going well, and I was getting out to help. We published a guidebook for tourists. We depended on selling advertising for our business. I would do a little of everything, including some of the selling. It felt good to be productive, to know I was contributing to the family income. I never had control over any of the money from the business, that was all his job, of course. I sold advertising, did some of the manual work making the ads, writing, drawing up maps, and putting our publication together on the computer. I helped with all of it, while taking care of my two girls, and our home.

Rachel had started kindergarten, and loved school. I signed her up for soccer, and we made some new friends. It was nice, they were all from different states, so we all had different accents, and attitudes. Rachel and the son of her soccer coach enjoyed sitting on the sidelines of the games, eating all of the orange slices, and mostly watched their team play. They were two peas in a pod. His mom and I began to talk a lot, at the games, and while we sat waiting for the kids to get out of school every day. She was from the northern part of the east coast, and I enjoyed talking to her. I loved her accent and her sense of humor.

One day we were sitting on a long bench outside the kindergarten class waiting for the kids. There were about twenty or so other parents sitting on the bench with us. I was listening to my friend talk, and out of the corner of my eye I happened to see a large man walking up. I was mostly struck by his size at first, and then I noticed he had overalls on, without a shirt, and he was barefoot. He had really large muscles, completely toned. My friend noticed him as well. There was something about him. As he walked closer to us, I noticed he may have had a bit of a mental challenge. He seemed lost. He kept walking towards us, and then I realized he was walking right up to me. I smiled, thinking he was going to talk to me.

Before I could say hello, he literally sat down on my lap! He reached down, grabbed my hands, and started clapping them together, really hard. He was extremely strong, and was such a large man, at this point I was in pain. Not only were my hands in pain, but my thighs were hurting just from the pure weight of him. This guy was really big, well over six feet tall. It lasted for a little while, and I was hoping someone would help me, I was hurting. Everyone just watched.

Suddenly, I heard a woman's voice, "David, what are you doing?" He didn't answer, he just kept slapping my hands together. "I bet nobody knows you are out here," she said kindly to him. She walked up and grabbed his hand and pulled him up to his feet, and led him down to the end of the building.

I just sat there, stunned. My eyes were filled with tears. My hands were burning, my legs were killing me, and what the heck was that? What just happened?

After a few moments of complete silence, my friend says, matter of factually, in her east coast accent, "well, you handled that very well, I have a problem with strange men touching me!"

I couldn't help but laugh, through my pain and tears. Touching me? I was sat on. A mountain of a man just sat on my lap. It was extremely bizarre.

Why me? Why did he choose me?

Chapter 7

Sometime after the strange incident with David, we decided to make a trip down to Texas. We would take two cars, so the girls and I could have an extended visit with my parents. They had only met Hannah once, when she was about four months old. She was nine months old now, and it killed me that they didn't know my baby. If my parents were anything, they were absolutely wonderful grandparents. I wanted my children to have a relationship with my parents, not just see them as people we visit once or twice a year. Rachel already had a relationship with them, and Hannah was going to have the same, but it would be difficult living a thousand miles away.

Before we moved to Colorado, I had envisioned trips down to Texas for visits, much more often than we were allowed. I never dreamed it would only be once or twice a year, but somehow I was not allowed to spend that money, or any money. Ron took all kinds of trips, deep-sea fishing in the Gulf of Mexico, a trip to New York City with a friend, wherever he needed to go. Sadly, for the girls and I to visit family, it was limited to once or twice a year.

Our trip was planned. Our first stop would be at Ron's parent's farm, which was in North Texas. We would stay a couple of days there, visit with them, and then drive down to central Texas to my parent's ranch. They had moved to the ranch after my dad's retirement. They had built a nice home, at about the same time I was in school getting my design degree, something I used to help with the planning of their new home. It had been exciting helping with the plans, helping them decide where to put lighting, or what finishes to use throughout the home. I had felt useful, and hoped my parents could be proud of my educated skills, after disappointing them so many times before.

I would get to stay an extra week with the girls and Ron would go back to Colorado for the business. We had just finished up our selling period, and had some time now to visit our families. Ron would always send me to different places to sell advertising because he felt like "They'll buy from a woman." I would go to these places, and I sold a few advertising spots, *only* because I was a woman, according to Ron. I sold a few on my own, and was still doing a good part of the computer work, making the ads, and laying them out in our publication. I did all of this work, but I still wasn't allowed to have access to any of the money. I was always supposed to live on whatever child support I got from Rachel's father, or I would have to get another job. This vacation time now was my escape.

We made it, in two cars, down to his family's farm in North Texas. It was a pretty place, surrounded by Cypress and Pine trees. There was a little lake in front of the little old house, which was part of the view from the front windows. His parents were standing outside waiting when we drove up.

We spent a couple of days there, and were to drive down to my parent's ranch the next day. I looked on a map to make sure I knew the way, and noticed where one of the towns on the route, was the little town Mark and Maggie were laid to rest. I realized it had been ten years since Maggie had passed, twelve for Mark. Ten years?

Twelve years? It couldn't be that long ago, I thought.

After looking at the map, it was on my mind for the rest of the evening. I wanted to go to the cemetery. I didn't tell Ron, and kept it to myself. I didn't need his opinion, or judgment. We were in two cars, and I knew he was going to leave later than I was, so I could stop there and he would never know.

The next morning I awoke early and started getting the girls ready, when Ron said he would keep Hannah with him. Of course.

I was so excited about the cemetery, and I knew I would lose any argument when it came to Hannah, so I let it be. Rachel would ride with me, and Hannah would go with Ron. It would be fine.

Rachel and I set out on our little adventure, left Hannah, which was always difficult, but that's just the way it was. We stopped to get drinks and snacks, and I filled my car with gas. I had my map sitting close. I told Rachel about the stop we would make, and she thought it sounded exciting. She was five years old.

We made our way through many towns, switched highways, and finally, after two and a half hours, I saw the sign I had been waiting for. We were almost there. The little town looked the same as I had remembered, maybe a few new businesses, but mostly the same. As I drove near the center of town I remembered the railroad tracks, and a street we had turned on, that I knew would lead us to the cemetery. It was a really small town, and there weren't many choices, so I knew I was on the right track.

There it was, perched atop the trees, the old rusted water tower . . . I remembered. I took another turn, and saw the wrought iron fence, lining the cemetery. I couldn't believe I had remembered everything, after so many years. The day of Maggie's funeral was so traumatic for me, the entire day was a blur. I could only remember little bits of the day, and here I was, ten years later.

I parked just outside the fence, near an opening, and we jumped out of the car. My heart was racing. I had remembered we all walked along that side, down a little dirt road, and were near some trees. Well, there were lots and lots of trees staring at me, and suddenly, all I saw were trees, and headstones. Maybe this was going to be a little more difficult than expected. I was losing a bit of confidence in my memory.

We walked where I thought we needed to be, and I was searching every stone for Mark's and Maggie's names, and couldn't find them anywhere. Rachel was following me, helping me search. We walked around for about ten minutes now, with no luck. I was beginning to get discouraged, and doubting my memory. I had been blessed with a good sense of direction, but my memory was wrong. Rachel began to wander, and I tried to keep track of her, as she began to get farther away, while I searched rows of names. I would call to her, and tell her to come back, but my little explorer wasn't listening.

I was feeling uneasy, discouraged, lost. Where are they? It had now been twenty minutes. No luck.

"Mommy!" Rachel called out to me. "Mommy, look at this kitty!"

Rachel was a known cat lover, and she had found a cat. I walked over to her, and saw the cat standing at her feet, rubbing against her legs, asking for attention. She reached down to pet the cat.

"Be careful," I said, "we don't know that kitty."

This was a distraction. I needed to get back to my search, it had now been almost thirty minutes. I told her to follow me, I had to keep looking. I went back to the car to start over. Maybe I had just missed something. The cat was meowing so loudly and Rachel couldn't leave it alone. She began to follow the cat back into a different area, and I was following them. Frustrated. Still searching. I was becoming certain I was in the wrong area now. We were just following the cat, wasting our time.

"Mag-gie," Rachel said. "Here she is."

I looked up. There they were. I couldn't believe it. A wind blew up, leaves blew up in the air gently. Chills went up and down my body. There they were. I could not believe we found them.

There they were.

Mark and Maggie.

We sat down at the foot of their graves, and the cat crawled into Rachel's lap.

The cat. That cat led us right to them.

We sat quietly. I was there, with them, after so many years. I hoped they saw my girl. I hoped they knew we were there. I felt like they did, but I hoped.

It was emotional, but I was so glad I had come here, it was comforting. It felt right. I missed my friends. In my mind I was telling them I missed them, and that I was so sorry. Apologies I never had the chance to give when they were alive. Guilt. I still felt guilt. It was a little sad seeing their graves were empty of flowers, and there was no sign of any visitors. Ten years, twelve years ago, it didn't seem possible that so much time had passed, and it didn't seem fair that they weren't here.

We left after a little while, knowing Ron would be right behind us, and this had taken a lot longer than I had planned. Rachel wanted to bring the cat with us, and it took a few minutes to make her understand that the cat had a home nearby. I broke down and promised her a cat, someday.

As we drove for the next two and a half hours or so

to the ranch, I couldn't stop thinking about what we had just experienced. That crazy cat, leading us to their graves, the breeze that had blown up, all of it. I had felt something.

Everything went as planned. Ron and Hannah showed up soon after we reached my parent's, and we spent a few days enjoying seeing everyone. My sister and I had both given birth to baby girls, less than forty-eight hours apart, so Hannah and her cousin were exactly the same age. They were really cute together, opposites like my sister and I, but so adorable as a pair. Our oldest children were close in age as well, Rachel and my sister's son were beginning to develop a close bond, they were only a year and a half apart in age.

We hated to leave Texas again, it was always so much fun to spend time at the ranch, and being around family, but soon we were on our way back home. Our life in Colorado was growing. We were making friends, settling in, still trying to deal with the cold and snow. I had never dreamed the snow would interfere with my every-day activities the way it did.

There is a big difference between vacationing in Colorado, and living in Colorado, I discovered. When you vacation, you really don't get a feel for shoveling two feet of snow from your doorstep and sidewalk, like you do when you live there. I had to learn the hard way to carry different gadgets in the car, just in case the quiet snow decided to bury your car while you were inside a store, grocery shopping. I came out of the store one day with the girls, and a full basket of groceries, only to find our car under eighteen inches of snow. My respect for people in the North grew at that time, I had never understood how much extra work wintertime was!

Boulder was a beautiful place to live, but

outrageously expensive, compared to what we were used to in Texas. In order to buy a home, we had to move closer to Denver, which we eventually did, about a year and a half after we moved to Colorado. The girls and I were down in Texas for a long awaited visit with my family again, when Ron called and informed me that he and his mom had bought a house for us. What? A home? You did it without me? You actually bought a house without me?

I was disappointed I had not been included in the purchase of our home, actually more than disappointed. I was hurt and insulted. This was shocking, even in our marriage. My mom was floored. My dad was shocked. My friends said that this was cause for divorce!

I asked where our new house was located.

"It's in your brother's neighborhood, but it's way on the other side, you go in through a different entrance," he said.

This was all the information I had at this time, it was all I knew about our new home. I didn't want to go back to Colorado. I didn't want to leave the ranch, where I felt safe, and somewhat important. I extended our visit as long as I could, but eventually had no choice but to return and face reality, face the life someone else had chosen for us.

The girls and I flew back to Colorado a few weeks later, ready to see our new home. Ron drove us over to see the house immediately, and it was true, we went in a different entrance than we normally would to get to my brother's house. When I walked inside, I went straight to the kitchen, looked out the window, and looked directly at the back of my brother's house, one block away.

"Ron, you know that's their house, right there?" I asked.

He acted like this was a complete surprise. I knew

my brother's wife would be angry. He knew she would be angry. This was invading her space. She had openly expressed her feelings about family many times before. She liked distance from family. I was afraid she would be angry at me, even though I had no control over the situation. The first chance I got, I explained to her what had happened, and apologized. There was nothing else I could do at that point.

The house itself was cute. It was a multilevel home with a basement, something I was appreciating about the homes in Colorado. I would finally have room to store everything, and a space for the kids to play during bad weather. The landscaping was beautiful.

I was grateful to have a nice home, but I was feeling very unimportant. I didn't have any power in this marriage, the business, or even choosing our home. I would do my best to make it feel like a home.

The day after we moved in, Ron had to go out of town. This was normal behavior, and I was getting used to it. I was surrounded by boxes, trying to keep my girls occupied while I unpacked, and he was gone. Our "normal."

That same day our neighbors were having a block party, which we joined for a little while. We met a few neighbors and Rachel even made a new friend. It gave me a new energy to get the house unpacked and organized, for the most part. This house, this home, that was not mine.

Since living in Colorado, my thoughts often went back to my experiences with Mark and Maggie. There was an attitude there about paranormal activities, psychics, metaphysical ideas, everything New Age, that I had never experienced before. It was everywhere. I had been told before that I was psychic, and clairvoyant, but I really didn't know what to think of what had happened to me. I started to do some research, and dabbled with the idea of writing a book. I felt a yearning to get it out on paper, and maybe try to make sense of something.

I met an artist, became friends with her, and she inspired me to do more creative things. I had always missed being in art class in high school, and college, and missed the release of all of my creative energy. I just hadn't had the moment of peace to do anything about it. I still played piano, which was a source of joy for me, and also a stress release at the end of a day. I wanted to paint, wanted to create something, and wanted to write.

We did enjoy getting out into the mountains, also, and took advantage of everything being so close to us. We spent many days driving through Estes Park, and exploring picturesque mountain towns like Grand Lake, my favorite place in Colorado. The first time we went there I spotted a house across the lake, and pictured myself sitting inside typing out a novel, overlooking the beautiful lake and mountains.

Ron's parents eventually moved back to Texas, but they still owned our home. Not us, and certainly not me. I was grateful we were living in such a nice home, but I never felt like it was "my home." Never. It was thrown in my face quite a few times, especially when I voiced an opinion, or argued with Ron.

When Hannah was about eighteen months old, I was sitting at the dining room table sewing matching dresses for the girls. She walked up suddenly and kicked me really hard in the leg.

"Hannah!" I exclaimed, "that hurt, why did you do that?"

She stood there, completely still, tears in her eyes, a pacifier in her mouth, just staring at me. She didn't move. Ron came walking up behind her, and said "she's mad at me because I told her no."

It was bizarre. I didn't know what to think. This was not like Hannah, to be this aggressive towards me. Most of the time, especially around other people, Hannah would want me to hold her. I picked her up and tried to create some kind of distraction, and really didn't think too much about it, other than how bizarre it was.

A couple of weeks or so later, I was outside with the girls, and they were playing with some little girls across the street. I was talking to one of the mom's, when another neighbor walked up. She told me she was a child psychologist. We began talking while we watched our girls play. She suddenly told me that Hannah "seemed to have a lot of anger inside of her."

I thought this was crazy. What kind of anger could a toddler have? I couldn't fathom such a thing, especially since she didn't want for anything, ever. Every need she had was met, always. My sweet little Hannah, angry. I couldn't believe it, or maybe I didn't want to believe such a thing. I guess I thought it might be a bit of an insult, to a certain degree, that our child had something really wrong with her. Another part of me wondered if she was looking for something wrong *because* she was a psychologist. I really didn't think about it too much after that day.

Chapter 8

Within four months of each other, my parents were both diagnosed with cancer. My father had stomach cancer, and my mother, breast cancer. It was a hard blow to all of us, but I couldn't sit still in Colorado, and not be able to be with them through this trying time. I wanted to be there to help them in some way. I wanted to help take care of them, but couldn't since I lived so far away.

I knew stomach cancer was a "fast" cancer, and it terrified me. They were to both have surgeries, and mom went through hers and did fantastic. My dads was scarier, they were to remove his entire stomach and "make a new one" out of the intestines. It sounded insane to me, and for many nights leading up to his surgery I did not sleep. Thankfully it went as planned, and soon they were both recovering well. We were all very relieved, and felt we were extremely lucky they were both going to be fine.

I took the girls down for a visit, and Hannah had a hard time recognizing my parents, and didn't feel comfortable around them right away. This was so sad to me because my family was everything I had.

During this particular visit, there were many discussions about my sister and one of my brothers moving to the ranch. My brother and his family would move into the "old" ranch-house we had all enjoyed in the past. My parents would help my sister build a home for her and her children. My parents offered to help build a home for me and my little family, as well.

We all realized how fortunate we were that my parents had seemingly both beat cancer, and this opportunity of living close to each other sounded like a dream. Time with my parents was even more precious now. The ranch had always been a "second home" for us, and we truly enjoyed spending time together as a family. This move made sense.

I didn't know how Ron would react when I discussed moving back to Texas, and was relieved when he agreed to move. Over a few short weeks we chose a site for our new home, and had a set of plans for a house to build. Ron would put our house in Colorado up for lease, and rent it out until his parents decided what they wanted to do with the home.

It would be so nice to be around my family for a while, and my kids could grow up with their cousins. Spending more time with my parents after both of their illnesses was my number one priority, and especially so my girls would have more memories with them.

We were set to move, everything was planned, and I had almost packed the entire house, by myself, of course. One week before moving day, almost packed and with a truck rental confirmation, Ron tells me he's not going. He would move us to Texas, but he wasn't going to live there.

What?

He decided he was going to stay in Colorado, and not move. He would just go back and forth, commuting here and there. I was upset. I was embarrassed to tell my parents after the planning we had done. Our business had a few weeks of down time every three months. It was the way it worked with our publication, we worked on a quarterly schedule. His new plan was to stay in Denver during selling times and come down to the ranch for a couple of weeks afterwards.

This was how we lived for four years. We had a new "normal." He had a life in Colorado, and we were building a new life in Texas. (It's just the way it was.) In order to spend time with my family, and let my children know their grandparents and cousins, this is how we would live.

The girls and I made a life quickly, and enjoyed our new home very much. We were out in the country, and with so many people in the family around, there was always something going on. It was busy, and fun. We did all kinds of things in town, and made some good friendships with some really great people.

It felt more like home than anywhere else we had ever been. Rachel was in second grade, and as soon as Hannah was old enough for preschool I found a job with an architect. He was well-known and respected by many in the town, and a very talented architect. He did all of his work on the computer, and at the time I was still drafting by hand. He quickly taught me the software program, and soon I was drafting on the computer. I was feeling a new confidence again, actually using the skills I had learned and worked for. I loved feeling productive. I worked on the third floor of an old historic building right on the town square, overlooking the courthouse in town. It was perfect.

After a while I was being sent out on job sites. One of my favorite jobs was going out on site to an old church in a little neighboring town, to measure a large section of the building that my boss was going to remodel. It took a few days to measure and record everything, but I really enjoyed crawling around that old church taking measurements. I would then go back to the office and enter all the information into the computer, and into the set of plans.

I finally felt like I was doing something productive, and the freedom I was experiencing gave me a new breath of life. The best part about the job was that I only worked until my children were out of school, so I could be with them for the rest of the day. It was a perfect fit for me and my girls, and we were happy. My marriage was still a mess, which would always find a way to spill into the life the girls and I had going.

Finances were a struggle, always. Ron came home to live with us again, after four years of commuting. He got a job with an insurance company in claims, which allowed him to work from home. He was out on jobs sometimes during the day, but his office was in our study at home. I would ask him to help pay the electric bill since his office was in our home, but he would say no. (He would tell me he bought a car for me, and that was enough.) I had no power, no voice, but lots of bills.

At one point I asked if we could go to marriage counseling, and he said I was the one with the problem, so I should go. I really felt trapped, and I was still too embarrassed to tell my parents, although I know they could see for themselves. I was struggling.

From the outside, I thought we looked fairly normal, except for a husband that sometimes lived somewhere else. I thought a lot of people have to do that, so it didn't seem all that strange. The architect I worked for jokingly said one day, "your husband must have another family, to be away so much." The thought had crossed my mind, and the sad part is that I probably wouldn't have cared much.

On the inside, I knew this was not normal at all, but I was determined to find a way to not get a divorce, another divorce. If I mentioned divorce to Ron, he would tell me if I divorced him he would take my children away from me. I really didn't know how in the world he would manage to take my kids, but something inside of me knew he could. I just had to keep going, I had no choice. The threat of him taking my kids, even though I had no idea how, was enough.

Ron's father became very ill. He had been through several illnesses and surgeries, but this time it was really bad. We went to Houston when he was placed in Hospice care at home. They said it could be a couple of days, or two weeks. They didn't know for sure, but it was going to happen. He was at the end. We stayed for a couple of days, and Father's Day came. Ron decided his dad was going to last for a few more days, so he was going to take us back home to the ranch, and he would go back to Houston to be there with his parents.

We packed our things, and I walked into the room where his dad was lying in bed. I was going to tell him goodbye. When I looked at his face, this strange feeling came over me. I quickly went to find Ron. I told him we shouldn't leave, I thought his dad was about to die, like in a few minutes. I didn't know how I knew. I don't think he believed me, but he went and told his mom. She quickly came into the room with us, and we sat and watched his father take his last breaths. It was Father's Day.

We finally drove home after getting things taken care of, and he made sure his mom was settled as much as possible. It had been a few days since his dad had passed, and we were talking to my dad, back at the ranch. He was catching us up on things that had been going on there, just conversation. He happened to mention one of his cows was down, and wouldn't get up. This usually meant they were ill, and would die unless you could get them up on their feet. If they stood up, sometimes they could get well, and miraculously be fine. We were curious, and wanted to see for ourselves, so Ron and I drove out to take a look at the cow.

As we drove around to a little meadow, or opening, on the other side of our creek, we saw the cow lying in the grass. We parked the truck away from her so we didn't frighten her, and slowly walked up to her. She wasn't lying on her side, she was just down, her legs tucked underneath her body. Her head was up. Ron thought maybe he could go get my dad's tractor and help her up, and was starting to make a plan. I looked at her eyes, and once again, a very strange feeling came over me. Her face had the same "look" that Ron's dad had, moments before he passed. She rolled on her side. I told him she was about to die. Sure enough, we stood there and watched that cow take her last breaths.

I was freaking out at this point, on the inside. I could not grasp what was going on. I couldn't understand why, in the last week, twice I have witnessed death, and even more disturbing, I saw it coming. I can't even describe the look on their faces, but it was the same. It was in their eyes, and the feeling I had was the same.

Ron called me the "angel of death." I thought maybe he was right. There was something wrong with me. I had always known that. All the memories of Mark and Maggie came back, and I began to feel really confused again. Whenever I felt this way, I would start researching any kind of weirdness, clairvoyant ability, psychic ability, all the stuff I thought was happening, that people had actually told me was different about me. I had always assumed it was something abnormal, but in a bad way. Always something negative. It was usually about death, so in my mind, it meant that I was morbid.

Every time I did my research it was always the

same, no answers. I wanted to write about my experiences and would start writing, but I could never find a direction. I would get it going, write about one hundred pages or so, and quickly hate everything I had written. The research did not help much, it would confuse me more. I could never figure out what was happening to me. I couldn't seem to find any answers. I read pages and pages of opinions from doctors and scientists, dismissing anything I had experienced, calling it impossible. I was simply the "angel of death."

After Ron's dad passed away, I felt even more grateful my dad had survived his stomach cancer. He was doing very well afterwards, and my children were able to make many memories with him. He was a fantastic grandfather. He would take all the kids to the nearby town, a tiny town with only a post office, hardware store, and a feed store. They would come home from the feed store with their own little brown paper bag full of candy, and a life-long memory. He spent a lot of time with all of them, and they loved him very much. Both of my parents had close relationships with almost all of their grandchildren.

My dad even made our dog's life more wonderful. Every day when we would all go to town for the day for school and work, our Golden Retriever would spend the day with him and his dogs, working around the ranch. Our houses were close, and every morning our sweet girl would hear him start his truck, and run down the driveway to meet him. He would stop the truck, allowing her to jump into the back with his two dogs. He would drop her off back at our house at the end of the day, and she was always exhausted. It was a good life, even for our dog.

My dad traveled around the world with his job

throughout my childhood, and I was enjoying living so close to him now. I was in my early thirties at this point, and I remember one day he came to my front door with somewhat of an odd request. He asked if I could drive his truck while he stood in the back, he was going to try and kill the coyote who had been terrorizing us, and our pets. We had named the coyote Wyle E., after the famous coyote of cartoon world, because he had become very bold and unafraid of our constant yelling and gun shots. He would come up to our fences in our yard, trying to get our cats, dogs, chickens, whatever he could grab, and he was not afraid to get close to us.

I dropped everything, and jumped in the driver's seat of the truck. We saw him out in the field, and my dad told me to get as close as possible. As I began to get slightly close, he would run quickly in a different direction. There were bumps and holes to watch out for, and chasing a wise coyote was more difficult than it might sound. I could see in the rear-view mirror that my dad's body was getting tossed around a bit, and I was afraid to drive too fast. I would hear a gun shot, and see the coyote change direction, and again, try to catch up to him. We were zigzagging left and right all through the field, and I was thinking, how many girls have *this* father-daughter experience? I'm guessing, not many. The whole situation was starting to be hilarious, with every missed shot. We were being humiliated by a coyote. I was giggling and driving, knowing that I was one very lucky girl. We tried for a couple of years to get Wyle E., but he was too smart and quick.

Living on the ranch was full of outdoor adventure, projects, and family togetherness. We had a good life. I don't think I had ever been so happy. Friday nights were the best. There were so many of us living on the ranch and we would all meet down at my brother's house and talk and laugh all night long. Our kids were able to have close relationships with their cousins, and were always together. They had something really special.

My family didn't believe in hiring other people to do work that you could do yourself. For the most part, this is an admirable principle, but sometimes our projects were a little overwhelming. There were many projects where we all would pitch in and help, even the kids. It was a good way to raise our kids. Everybody had to help.

One day I drove down to visit my brother and sister-in-law, their house was about two miles down the road on a different section of the ranch. As I drove up I noticed my brother on his tractor, out in the back yard. I saw he was digging an enormous hole with the tractor, and I could see him, and the tractor, disappear down into the ground as I drove up. I walked into the house, and asked my sister-in-law what in the world he was doing.

"He decided to make a swimming pool," she said.

Soon there we all were, the entire family, out in the Texas heat, over one hundred degrees, building a pool. The day the cement trucks came was the hottest day of them all, and we worked all day long in the sun. I was standing in the shallow end of the pool, and my brother told me I was in charge of building the steps. It seemed at that moment like an overwhelming task, and I took it very seriously. I had never worked with cement before, but in our family, this did not matter. We could do anything.

Suddenly, here came the truck, with a large arm on the back, and wet cement began to pour out quickly right in front of me. It was an enormous "blob" of wet cement. Somehow, I was supposed to transform this blob into the "steps," before the cement began to harden. I felt a lot of pressure to get it right.

I worked and worked, sweat pouring out of me, until it resembled steps. It was so hot we would take the water hose and just hold it over our head, until we were drenched, and it would cool us off for a little while. After a couple of hours, the steps were done. I was proud. This was our family, all working together, at that time in our lives we were a family.

Chapter 9

Six years after my dad's stomach surgery, he was going back into surgery for a new heart-valve. He was in his seventies now, and it would be a little tougher surgery. Everyone else I knew that had this surgery had a new breath of life, a new energy about them. Other people told me their fathers were almost "young again" after their surgeries. I was so excited for him, I wanted him to feel young again, feel good again. Unfortunately, my dad never felt young again, or even had a new breath of life. His body was worn out. He was still really down.

A few months after his surgery, I became pregnant. I had lost a pregnancy almost two years before and didn't think I'd ever get pregnant again, but it happened. The girls and I were so excited, we wanted a baby more than anything. I think in the back of my mind, I thought it would stop the division in our family. Whenever Ron was home, either to live with us or visit for the weekend, we were split into two families. He and Hannah were the first and most important, and Rachel and I were the second. I always wanted a large family, and was so excited to have another baby. This was just what we needed.

I was about two months away from giving birth, when my dad fell ill. He wasn't doing well. I took him to the doctor for a blood test. I had to help him walk because he was so weak, and they admitted him into the hospital.

Almost two weeks later my family and I were all standing on the lawn of the hospital watching him being carried away by helicopter to a bigger hospital in Austin. I could see on his face he was tired. He looked defeated and exhausted. He didn't look like himself. He was always strong, and going all day long, with energy to last. We had always joked that he was the Energizer Bunny.

I wanted him to hold on until he could meet my new baby. I talked to a friend, and she told me she asked God to take her own father when he was dying, if it was his time, but heal him if it wasn't. I remember thinking I couldn't bear to lose my dad, and wasn't sure if I could ask God to take him. I did what she said, but I didn't mean it. I wanted my dad to stay and live and meet my baby.

The next week was spent in ICU, trying to not lose hope. Our super-man was going down. We walked into the room one day, with my mom, and my dad looked up at her and said "I'm not going to make it." She quickly replied back to him, "yes you are." The very next day, it was over. We lost. I felt like I lost everything. I couldn't breathe.

No. Just no. Not my dad.

My world went dark.

No. Just no.

I had never felt so fragile in my entire life. Every feeling, every nerve, every emotion literally on the outside of my body, completely unprotected. I felt like everything had been ripped out from under me. I could not believe my dad was gone.

Six weeks later, I gave birth to another beautiful baby girl. She was our joy. She was our new everything. Life was feeling as good as possible, considering, even though my heart was broken. I still felt incredibly fragile, and vulnerable from the loss of my dad, but this sweet little baby was bringing so much happiness to the girls and I, and to my mom. It felt like she was sent to mend our hearts. She was our world.

Our new baby, Lizzie, was born with severe re-flux, which made it a little difficult to leave the house, but we managed. She would get sick about eight to ten times every day. The girls started school again when Lizzie was four months old, and we were still struggling with her re-flux. I would take the kids to school in the morning, and try to get Lizzie back home as quickly as possible, in case she was going to become ill. If I heard one tiny little choking sound coming from the back seat, I would pull my van over quickly, and get her out of her car seat as fast as I could.

When we got back home every morning, I would put towels down on the bed, and we would spend our day there. I would set her in a little sling chair, to keep her at a certain angle, and I would feed her, entertain her, love her. At night she slept in the sling chair on my bed, next to my pillow, and I would build a wall of pillows on the other side of her. This was our life for about seven or eight months. The end result was a healthy baby, and a bond between us like no other.

Ron had moved again to live with his mom in Houston just after Lizzie was born. We managed to have a routine, even with a new baby, without him. He would call occasionally, and come to visit us every once in a while, but he really wasn't there much during Lizzie's infancy.

The girls were very motherly towards Lizzie, they each felt that she was their baby. Hannah was so protective of her, she wouldn't let go of Lizzie when she was trying to learn how to walk. I had to tell her to let her fall a little bit, so she could learn *not* to fall. Hannah was only nine when Lizzie was born, Rachel was fourteen.

Lizzie basically had three mothers. This baby was very loved.

The division in our little family did not end, like I had hoped it would. Ron still took Hannah off for visits with his mom, he would take her off for the day when he was home. Most of the time it was just the three girls and I and it was actually just fine, we had our own lives. He still came home to live with us some of the time. We adjusted to whatever came our way.

We were always known as "Jen and the girls," wherever we went. I remember talking to some friends at a school function one time, and I mentioned my husband. One of my friends, whom I had known for about two years, looked at me funny, and asked, "You're married?" It's just the way it was. Several of my friends would occasionally ask how I could possibly let my husband live away from us so much. My answers were always the same, "I don't know any other way," while thinking to myself, "because I have no power, and I don't really matter."

I would study other couples I knew, and the "good" couples who really seemed to love each other, well I thought they were simply "lucky." I thought maybe I wasn't a lucky person. Most of these lucky people I knew were all very involved in their churches, their communities, and I even noticed their children had a certain quality that I wanted my children to have. I really wasn't comparing myself to them, it was more like trying to figure out how to live like them. I did my best, on my own with the girls, but we weren't a complete family. I wanted it for my girls. I wanted them to feel like they had a good family.

Chapter 10

A year before I had Lizzie, my sister also had her third child, a boy. He was the sweetest little boy. When Lizzie was almost two years old, I was keeping him for my sister a few days a week while she was at work. It was only temporary, but we enjoyed it very much. I had a part-time job, and on the days I worked, Lizzie was now going to preschool at a church in town. He and Lizzie were really sweet together, they really loved each other. They never fought, they shared, and they were fun to watch. They would watch Dora the Explorer together, play with Lizzie's toys, sit and eat together, like best friends, never once arguing or fighting. My sister and her husband were getting a divorce, and her son went to stay with his dad for the summer, so we didn't get to see him for a while.

It was almost the end of summer, the very beginning of August. Ron was home, and we had decided to go to Austin and stock up on some supplies. We spent the day shopping. We went to Home Depot, Target, out to lunch, and our last stop, Sam's Club. We were going to buy food, especially meats that we could freeze. We were tired as we left Austin, but had to hurry home to get the food into the freezer. It was August, in Texas, and very hot.

I was driving the van, Ron was in the passenger seat, and all of the girls were in the back. We drove for half an hour to Lockhart, which was half-way home. Just as we were leaving Lockhart, I was on the road that would take us home, and suddenly a State Trooper appeared on my left, passing me, going really fast. It scared me, because I didn't see him until he was right beside me. Ron said there was probably a wreck up ahead somewhere, because they send Trooper's to accidents. He disappeared out of sight quickly. This feeling suddenly came over me, and I couldn't figure out what it was, and I kept it to myself. I could feel it all over my body, even my face. The only way I can explain the feeling is a strange "tickling" literally all over my skin, all of my muscles tense slightly, and deep inside there was a feeling of "knowing."

We drove the long stretch of the road along fields of cotton, little farmhouses, and oil derricks. After the long, straight stretch, came the curves. This road was a constant sequence of "S" curves, really dangerous, and just two little narrow lanes. It was one curve after the other. After we had driven for about fifteen minutes, through almost all of the curves, I saw two women up ahead waving their arms, trying to tell us to stop.

I slowed down and came to a stop right in front of them. This feeling was growing inside of me, getting more intense. They informed us that there was a really bad wreck just ahead, around the curve. We couldn't see anything, but they said it was "really, really bad."

I suddenly knew what it was, this horrible feeling.

"It's my sister," I blurted out.

"I know it's my sister," I said it again.

We just sat there for a moment. Ron asked me if I wanted to try to drive closer and see if it was her. Before the women could tell us no, I said no, I needed to get home quickly.

I just knew my sister had been seriously injured, or worse. I needed to get home, to help my mom. I felt a feeling of death.

Rachel cried out, "What's wrong with you, mom?"

She was scared. She was aware of some of the weird experiences I had in the past. I had shared everything with her. I didn't know how I knew, I didn't know what was *wrong* with me. I just knew, with certainty, it was my sister, and it was bad.

I put the van in reverse, and turned around to go find another way around. Everyone was quiet after that. I found another dirt road, and hoped it would get me around to the highway, to get to our road that we needed. It worked. Soon we were back on the road, almost home. About another fifteen minutes, and we would be home, and I could help. There was a silent, tense feeling in the car.

Just as we were getting close to our front gate, my cell phone rang. It was my niece, my sister's daughter. She was eleven, same as Hannah.

"Jen?" I heard her little voice. "My mom got in a wreck."

"I know, we just drove up on the accident, is she okay?" I asked, hoping she would say yes, but still feeling death.

"We think she's okay, but we don't know about the baby." The baby. I didn't know she had the baby back from the summer visitation. The baby. He's almost three.

I told her to hang on, I was coming to help them. They were in Luling, already at the hospital, the wrong hospital. They had driven there thinking it was where the ambulance would take my sister and her son, because it was the closest town with a hospital. I would get there as fast as I could to drive them to the hospital in Austin, where they had actually taken my sister and her little boy.

We finally drove up to our house, and everyone

grabbed all the supplies, and food we had bought, and threw it up on the porch. We emptied the van in a minute, and I was headed to the hospital in Luling. We were all scared, and I could see it on my girls faces, but I had to leave, and fast. By the time I got there my mom and my sister's two oldest kids were walking out the front door to my van. I saw a friend of mine, Faith, walking behind my mom. Faith was a nurse at that hospital. My mom said Faith didn't know anything, either, so we still didn't know what condition they were in.

We knew nothing.

Faith calmly told me exactly where to go, and sent us on our way. It was almost an hour to the hospital. We drove with such a sad and scary atmosphere in the car. We talked about other things, anything other than what was happening, mostly to keep the kids calm. Her children were terrified. We were terrified. I felt so sad, and sorry for these kids, I couldn't believe this was happening to them. I was sad for my mom, she had just lost my dad, about two years earlier, and I could see she was still so fragile. We were all still fragile, still hurting over him. I wish my dad was here, I kept thinking, we needed my dad. My dad.

By the time we reached the front of the hospital in Austin, there was no parking. I dropped them off, told my nephew, now almost fifteen, to take care of my mom, his grandmother. They walked up to the door, and I was off to find a place to park.

I had trouble, and it took me a few minutes. I finally found a spot, got out and ran as fast as I could back up to the front door. I walked in, looked around in a panic, and couldn't find my mom and the kids anywhere. I went up to a desk, and asked where I could find my little nephew. I told them he had been brought in from an accident near Lockhart, and gave them his name. They were trying to find it in the computer. They couldn't find it. They tried again, and one more time. There was something wrong, they weren't looking in the right place, I thought. I started to think we were in the wrong place. I was getting really scared at this point, and didn't see my family anywhere.

My cell phone rang. It was my niece again. Oh, good, I thought, she'll tell me where they are. I answered, and stepped away from the desk.

"Jen . . . the baby didn't make it," she cried.

What? What did she say?

No. Just no. No. No. No!

My knees gave out. I fell to the floor. I couldn't breathe. Two people walked up and picked me up and dragged me into a little room off to the side. They helped me up onto an examination table.

I tried to talk. I couldn't catch a breath. I was trying to tell them I needed to find my family. I was telling them this baby was the sweetest child. Did they realize this was the sweetest little boy you could ever meet? I had always told everyone that, and it's all that came out of my mouth at this moment. He was so sweet. His soul was sweet.

No, just please no.

I finally caught my breath, and felt like I could walk. One of the nurses led me to a room down in another section of the hospital, where a social worker would be talking to my family. It was surreal. I finally saw the kids, and my mom, sitting, all stunned, in this tiny little room. My poor mom. Those poor kids. My sister walked in and she was all banged up, blood on her skirt, and some large bandages all over her. My poor sister. I couldn't believe this was happening. But it was.

Just no.

He really was gone. We had to go home, without him. It was so hard to leave that hospital, knowing he was not coming with us. That was it. That sweet baby boy was gone. Gone.

By the time I was driving everyone home, it was late at night. We had to get my mom's car from Luling, which was a much longer route home, but the best way. It would keep us away from the accident site. I wanted to stay as far away from that road as possible. As we drove, my sister was in the passenger seat which was tilted almost all the way back. She slept.

They had given her medications, and thank goodness, she was sleeping. I drove as slowly and as carefully as I could. We were all quiet. There were no sounds. Everyone was in shock. Suddenly she jumped, and screamed "watch out, this curve is dangerous, you'll roll the car." It frightened all of us.

We were on a very straight, flat highway. She was traumatized, and re-living the accident. As quickly as she had jumped up and screamed, she laid back down to sleep. It was intense. The kids began to cry, and I was trying hard to focus on not waking her again. I was trying my best to get there without hitting any bumps. I made it all the way to Luling, driving as slowly as possible over the railroad tracks, and ever so slightly turned right at the stop light. My van was barely moving, as I turned at the light, because I didn't want to make any sudden stop. I was still driving slowly, about to turn onto the street that the hospital was on, and suddenly, I see flashing lights behind me.

I was being pulled over. I gently stopped in front of the H-E-B grocery, and got out of the van as quickly and quietly as I could. I saw the officer getting out of his car, and I was walking up to him, and he started yelling at me.

"Get back in the vehicle!" he screamed.

"But officer, I need to talk to you out here," I tried to tell him. "Please," I asked as politely as possible.

Again, he screamed at me, "Get back in the vehicle!"

Over and over, as I tried and tried to tell him about what had happened to us, trying to make him understand. I only wanted to let my sister rest. He just kept screaming, until I was backing up to the driver's door of my van. I was frustrated. I was trying to tell him the situation, that my sister had been in the accident this afternoon around Lockhart, because I was sure he had heard about it. He didn't seem to care, and just kept screaming. I was just about to open my door and get back in the van, when I heard a voice behind me.

"Jennifer?" the voice called.

I turned around.

There was Faith. Walking up out of the dark.

"Jennifer, do you need help?" she asked.

"Yes, he won't let me explain, he just keeps screaming at me. My sister's in the car," I told her.

She immediately went into action. Sweet Faith.

"Officer, this family has had a tragedy this evening. What is your badge number?" is all I heard her say.

I knew it would be okay now. Relief. My angel, Faith was here. She had literally walked up out of the dark and saved me. I knew it had to be God that had sent her. I just knew. All I was trying to do was let my sister rest, that was all. I had been driving so slow, and careful, and doing what I thought I was supposed to do.

Faith settled it with him, and we were able to get back on our way. We couldn't believe what had happened. We still had about a twenty minute drive home after we picked up my mom's car.

We finally got home, and the shock was still there. Nobody slept. We were all on the phone all night long, back and forth. News had spread throughout the family quickly. The next day was a blur, and the funeral was planned. None of us could grasp it all. He was just a baby, nobody should have to bury a sweet little child.

We had his funeral on his third birthday. It was the saddest day. I kept hoping, and wishing he was with my dad, bouncing on his knee. That is the only way I could deal with it, thinking of my dad holding him in Heaven, or whatever was on the other side. I knew they had to be together. I missed my dad so badly, and I wanted to know they were together. I *needed* to know they were together. All I could do was hope. I thought about Faith, and how I felt at that moment she walked up out of the dark, and rescued me. I had felt like God sent her. It had to be God, I thought. It had to be God, but I still didn't know how I knew any of the things I knew, or had felt that night. I wanted to believe, more than anything, I really did.

Just like before, I had something happen that couldn't be explained, and I wanted answers. Was I psychic? Was it God? I was still "on the fence" about God, not having any knowledge, and being very uneducated. I couldn't make any sense of anything that had happened, once again. Total confusion.

This tragedy actually divided my family, and we would never be the same. Things were never really the same after my dad had passed, and this tragedy only widened the separation. Only a handful of our family showed up to the funeral, neither one of my brother's attended, it was just too much for them, I guess. One of our nieces from Houston drove out for the service, and my little family was there. My mom, my sister and her two older children, and a handful of friends, and others were there. I don't remember much from that day, only an incredible sadness. A sadness came over me that was progressing as the days went by. Our family was split in two. My dad was no longer here to make things better. So much sadness.

In the following days we were all dealing with it the best way we could, trying to go on with life. School would start, and things would get back to "normal". I worried about my sister. She had just experienced and lived my own worst nightmare, losing a child. I worried about my mom, another heartbreak, so soon after losing her husband of fifty-three years. I worried about my niece and nephew, they had lost their baby brother, it was all too much.

I tried hard to stay strong and be there to help, but I felt myself dying inside. My sister would call at night, and she would go over and over the accident, reliving it every day. It was horrible. I could see it on my face in the mirror. I was going down. There was too much sadness.

After a few months, we went down to Corpus Christi to visit my eldest brother. He had just moved his family from the ranch, to Corpus, to take a new job. They had a large, beautiful home, right across from the water. We felt so good being near the water, and I was so miserable on the ranch now, surrounded by nothing but sadness and grief.

I struggled with the idea of leaving the ranch, moving, and at first couldn't fathom such a thing. The ranch was my home. It was our home. It held no joy anymore, and was a place of despair for me now. We felt refreshed in Corpus Christi. Every time we drove down there to visit, the minute we would get to the big bridge, we would roll down all of the windows. The salty gulf air was like a drug, with healing power. It felt incredible.

Rachel was in her junior year of high school, and I asked her what she thought about moving down to the coast. I thought I'd let her decide, since she was at such a crucial time in high school. She was a wonderful student, on the drill team, had a good circle of friends, and a social life. I was shocked when she said she would move in a heartbeat.

I asked Hannah, and she was just as excited. The girls both felt better in Corpus, as well, and we all needed healing. Now to ask Ron. He also agreed, which made the decision that much easier. It was settled. I had to move, I had to save myself. I was dying on the inside, and it was showing on my face. I was forty at that time.

I asked my brother if they could help us get a house, and I would sell my ranch house to pay him back as quickly as possible. He said he would help, and that is exactly what we did. We went down to look around, they bought a house for us, and I sold my beloved ranch house, and paid him back. It was done. We were living in Corpus Christi. The emotional struggle was there, and I felt like I had abandoned my mom and sister. But if I wasn't strong, and couldn't help them anyway, what good was I to them?

I had to save myself. I had to run. It was killing me to leave the ranch. Killing me to leave the place I had lived for ten years, around our family, but it was killing me more being there. All the memories of my dad and his love for the ranch and his family, the attachment I felt to him, we were leaving it all behind.

We never looked back. Our life changed, our hearts were trying to mend, and we had a whole new life, just like that.

Chapter 11

Corpus Christi. I couldn't believe we were living in Corpus Christi. I had sworn I'd never move, never leave the ranch, and here we were. The air was different. I could breathe. It felt good.

The girls transitioned very nicely. Rachel came home from the first day of school, telling me about her new group of friends, already. She was a butterfly, not shy. Her letter-man's jacket had been a topic of conversation the whole day, because it was full of colorful chenille patches. It wasn't the monotone scheme that most people had. It drew enough attention to break the ice. She was automatically accepted on the drill team, since she was on the team at her other school. She would do fine, I knew.

Hannah, on the other hand, was slower to make friends. She took her time, observed people, before taking the plunge. She was quiet, more reserved than her talkative sister. After the third day of asking her if she made any friends that day, she finally said she made one. I was relieved. It didn't take long for her to have a "group," she was just a bit more cautious than Rachel. It was the difference in their personalities. I knew she would be fine. Thank goodness.

Our Realtor recommended a good preschool for Lizzie and I enrolled her immediately. It was a Christian preschool, fairly close to our home. Lizzie could adapt to any situation, any group of people. She loved her new school. I knew she would be fine. Lizzie and I actually loved driving to her school every morning, because we could drive along Ocean Drive, and see the bay.

I had always been an over-protective mother, since day one. I had seen so many people lose their children, and this became my biggest fear, since before I even had a child of my own. Hannah had come home from school one day when she was in third or fourth grade, and told me a friend at school had said "Hannah, you have a really good vocabulary." I asked her what word she had used to make her friend say this to her. "Paranoid," she said. I laughed, because I knew she had heard just about everyone in my family call me paranoid. Their kids would all run around, and not be "careful," and I was always hovering over mine, "be careful!"

Now, since the accident, I think I kicked it up into another gear, I was more fearful, more protective. Rachel was driving now, out there in the "world." I was terrified something would happen to her. I warned her about every little thing I could possibly think of that could possibly happen, just in case.

I think in my mind, I thought if I told her about all the possible threats, said them out loud to her, they wouldn't happen. It was a constant game my mind played, and everyone around me had to suffer. I still had the fear of my own thoughts since Mark and Maggie had passed away, so long ago. Being a mother now just amplified the fear, I now had so much more to lose.

Everyone was getting adjusted in Corpus, and I knew I had to find a job. Our Realtor, Jane, had become a friend of my brother and his wife, and I had started to make friends with her, as well. We hit it off immediately. She said real estate would be good for me, and I could come work for the company she worked for, and had worked for since they opened decades before. I had worked for an architect for years, and thought it might be a nice change to sell homes, instead of drawing them. I looked into it, and it was a possibility.

The next thing I knew I was sitting in my first real estate class. They were each one week long. I would take a total of five classes, and then take the real estate exam. It flew by, and I was relieved when I passed the exam. It was done. I was now a Realtor.

My heart was still broken, and guilt weighed heavily on me, for leaving my mom and sister, but this new life somehow felt right. It felt like it was where we were supposed to be. I began to feel the sadness lift a little, and I was coming back to life. I could even see a drastic difference in photos of myself. I had looked almost dead before, and now I was smiling and looked alive. I remember one of my nephew's took a picture of me with his phone one day, and when he showed it to me, all I saw were deep, dark lines, all over my face. It was scary, you could see the stress so clearly. These dark lines were now disappearing, and I felt like I was free again.

I called the real estate office, and made an appointment with the owner/broker, for an interview, just after passing the exam. I showed up a few minutes early, and he wasn't there. There was another woman there, another Realtor, Sara, and she was the only one in the office that day. We started talking, and talked, and talked. We had quite a lot in common, and she was sweet. We made friends immediately. She had four sons, and our kids were similar in ages. We were about the same age, grew up in the same time, and we just "clicked." Sara and I became the best of friends from day one.

I left, went back again later, and found out that the owner had forgotten our appointment. I hadn't minded, at all, I already felt comfortable in the office since I had been there earlier, which made the interview more relaxing. I had felt like I already had friends there, also, between Jane, and now Sara, it felt right.

I began working there soon after the interview. I was excited about this new career. New life. New everything. I loved living near the water, our house was less than two blocks away. Lizzie and I would go to the water after school, because she would want to "find Nemo," from her favorite movie. We would sit at the edge of the water, breathe in the gulf air, pretending to see a little Clown fish, Nemo, swimming around. The girls and I went to the beach as much as possible because it was only minutes away. It was our special time, a healing time.

Things were going great. I was working and the girls were doing great in school. We were spending a lot of time with our family there, my brother and all of his four children, all adults, and my brother's grandchildren. We spent many evenings and weekends at his home, sitting out around the pool, talking, just like old times at the ranch. Soon even more friends and family moved to Corpus. It was always fun. My kids were having a ball. We finally felt like we were "living" again.

Ron had a hard time finding work in Corpus, but my days were full. I would take the kids to school, go to work, go pick the kids up after school, except for Rachel, who had a car of her own now. We would all get home from our day, to begin our evening routine of dinner, homework, and any school activities. We were doing the "normal." We still couldn't believe we could get to a store in such a short time, and we joked about it every time. After living in the country for ten years, and driving sometimes well over one hundred miles a day, it was wonderful for everything to be so convenient now. The closest store to the ranch had been fifteen miles away, and their schools were anywhere from eighteen to thirty-five miles away. We were back in a city now, and the girls would say "it only took us eight minutes to get here, mom," or "it only took us two minutes and twenty seconds to get here, mom."

It was a whole new life for us, for sure. I just couldn't seem to shake the guilt, I still couldn't believe I had moved, again, and I certainly couldn't believe I had left the ranch. There was a constant fear that my dad was angry at me for leaving. I really hoped he could see how much better we were doing.

My thoughts drifted many times to the accident, and the fact that I had known it was my sister, somehow. I knew God had sent Faith to help me, but I thought it was a psychic ability that allowed me to feel my sister's situation. I was conflicted, and very uneducated. I was trying to figure it out all on my own, and I didn't get very far. At this point I was more confused than ever before. I needed answers.

The desire to write a book was always nagging at me, always in the back of my mind. I had written another hundred pages, and hated it. I could never get it together. I had all of these things happen, and wanted so badly to get them all out on paper. I still couldn't figure out the story, or the title, and I changed the whole point of the book many times. I changed the story, the characters, but it still wasn't right. In my many attempts at writing my story, I had always tried to write a novel. I tried to work my story into a novel with developed characters, and dialogue that would be crafted in such a way to enhance the story. It was a struggle. I would temporarily give up, and tell myself I'd try again, later. This had been going on for years. Over ten years.

I was becoming more frustrated in my marriage. No matter what I tried, nothing worked. Something was missing, that "thing" I saw in other couples. I had hung on now for twelve years, and nothing had really changed. My brother found a job for Ron, and he was off to another town, temporarily.

Then, another job, all the way up in Fort Worth. He told me the girls and I should move there. We were finally settled in Corpus Christi, and now he wanted us to move to Fort Worth? I couldn't do it, couldn't move again. I knew what it was like to live with him away from my family, it was all control, control, control. No thanks. Not again. I was just feeling some happiness again after all the tragedy, all the loss. The girls were happy, and enjoying living close to the beach, and the family. They had each found a group of friends that had accepted them, and I didn't want to risk moving again. Rachel was a senior, and going to graduate soon, so for her, moving wasn't even a possibility. He might not have that job for very long, anyway, I thought. There were plenty of reasons to stay right where we were.

Jane and I became closer, she was a little older, and after I "shadowed" her at work for a little while, we were close friends. I rode around with her for a couple of weeks, trying to learn as much as I could about the real estate business. She was an expert, had been selling real estate for over thirty years. I would always ride in the back seat of her car, because the front passenger seat was occupied with her dog's car seat. Her dog is her child, and she is probably going to get offended that I just called her child a dog!

She was such a delightful person, I could easily see that everyone loved her, and it was hard not to. She knew everyone in town, and had quite a large social and professional network. I loved her, and still do. We became very close friends. On one particular day, she was informing me of a trip to Houston she had to make. I had this unshakable feeling that I needed to drive her there myself. I couldn't get it out of my head, that I needed to drive her, and I told her what I was thinking. She was going to see her daughter and grandchildren. I had family and friends in Houston, and I thought the girls and I could stay with my family while she was visiting hers, and then we would drive her back home to Corpus. It was really bothering me, and I really felt this was something I had to do. I had prior engagements, and tried to get out of them, but couldn't. She left town on her trip.

I was just getting to the office, when the owner came over to me, and gently said he had some news. Jane was going to be fine, but she had been in an accident on her way to Houston. I couldn't believe it. I was so relieved she was going to be fine, her injuries were minor, but I was angry at myself for not driving her. I couldn't explain those feelings I had about her trip, and we talked about them for a long time. Jane couldn't believe it, either. It was another unexplained event, but luckily, this one had a better outcome. Maybe I wasn't the "angel of death," like Ron said.

At this time, Ron was coming home some weekends to visit. One particular weekend, he and I were to go out by ourselves, which was pretty unusual for us. We would go to play pool, which my whole family loved to do, and in Corpus there was a really nice place close by. We left our three girls together, at home. It was fun. We played a few games, had a couple drinks, good food, and stuffed a few dollars in the jukebox.

When we decided to play our last game and go home, he said he wanted to make a bet with me. Whoever lost the game had to do something the winner decided. I was a pretty good pool player, and I knew I could beat him if I did well. I figured the bet meant a back-rub, something simple, innocent. I took the bet. I scratched on the eight ball. I lost. Unfortunately.

We went to the car to go home, and while we were pulling out of the parking lot, he turns to me, and reminds me that I had lost the bet. I didn't really care, or really think about it.

"You lost, so you have to do something I tell you to do," he said.

Still thinking he'd want a back-rub, I said "okay, what?"

"I want to take you to a bar, and pick a man for you to make out with," he said.

What? Are you serious? Surely not.

"No," I said, hoping he was kidding.

He wasn't kidding. I was crushed. Insulted.

This is what I had hung on for, for twelve years?

You've got to be kidding.

I shook it off, and acted like it was a joke. I couldn't believe he wanted me to do such a thing. This meant he had no love for me. He didn't even love me at all. I had always thought there was some love in there somewhere, but now I knew the truth. I was crushed

The next day, I asked my brother, one of his friends, and his brother-in-law, all three, if they would want their wives to make out with another man in front of them. One said "hell no!" Another said "no." One didn't seem to care, really, or maybe he didn't understand the question, I wasn't sure.

I asked as many of my friends as I could, I just couldn't believe he had wanted me to do such a thing. I couldn't find anyone that would accept this from their own husband, but is this just how men are? Maybe there was something wrong with me, maybe this was acceptable behavior for others. I just couldn't stand the thought of watching anyone I love do something like this, especially not my husband!

You might not find anything wrong with his request, and I'm not trying to offend anyone here. Maybe you have done this in your own marriage, but given our history, this really crushed me.

I'm a romantic soul. This was not exactly the "chick-flick" story I was looking for. This was wrong, to me, and I could not believe he had even thought of such a thing.

I think it was the last straw for me. I was in my forties now, and life had once again thrown me a curve ball. I thought I had done the right thing for so long, hanging on to our marriage, and he didn't even love me at all. He was living in another city again, away from us. He wasn't helping us financially, again. He didn't love me, and was never going to change. I knew it was time. I had to get out of this marriage.

Now where can I get some courage? It's going to take some courage. He's threatened me before with taking my children away from me. I would reassure myself, tell myself there's no possible way he could actually do this.

Or was there?

My brother and his wife were encouraging me to file for divorce, and telling me I could find someone better, that I didn't have to live like this. They assured me, they would help me through. It felt like I had support. This would be the most terrifying thing, his threats were there, and my fear grew.

I decided I had to file for divorce. I walked into the attorney's office, downtown Corpus, an attorney someone had referred to us. I had the support of my brother, his wife, all of my friends, and my mother. I was really afraid, but this had to be done.

I am a casual person, and the office made me uncomfortable. It was too nice. Too expensive and shiny. I tried to focus. I sat and picked apart this design scheme in my head. There was nothing soft, or comfortable about the room. I was already terrified enough going to the appointment, and this atmosphere only made it worse.

By the time the receptionist said he would be with me in a few minutes, I was already extremely nervous. When I get nervous, tears start flowing. It's how I am wired. I told my story, as much as I thought he needed to know, and probably way more than he wanted to hear. When I get nervous, I cry, and talk a lot.

He would file the necessary papers and call me. Dates were set. This kind of talk gave me a headache. This was obviously not my strong suit. I had done this once before and knew the legal speak confused me, made me nervous. One little twist of a word and it's the opposite of what you think it is, all the double entendre's, it wasn't something I could handle.

I started to panic, thinking maybe I could just hang on a little longer in this marriage, maybe I can just live with it. I had done it this long. Is it too late? Wait a minute, what are you thinking? No, enough is enough. I went back and forth in my head a hundred times. I hated law. I hated fancy attorney's offices. I like the beach.

I was terrified.

I had to call Ron, now that everything was in motion. I needed to tell him, get it over with, and it was not going to be easy. My fear had grown into this monstrous-sized thing I could feel in my body. My kids, my kids. My babies.

I called him. I told him I had filed for divorce. The first thing out of his mouth, was a question, he wanted to know if we would be intimate again. What?

What in the world? I just filed for divorce, did you hear what I said?

Then he offered to hire a housekeeper for me. That would have been nice, I could have used the help.

Where was this offer before when I begged and begged for help? All I ever heard was the word "no." Every time I asked for anything, it was always no. If I argued at all, he would start telling me how stupid I was, or how my own family hated me, and how nobody really loved me, I was unlovable. Even my birth mother didn't want me, he said, and gave me away. You hear this kind of talk long enough, and it tends to wear you down. I admit, at this point in my life I was believing everything he was saying.

It was all happening, the second divorce I had tried not to have, for so long. I was a mess, again. He started coming to get the girls and taking them out of town to his mother's house in Houston. It was unbearable.

Rachel was going off to college, the girls weren't with me all the time anymore, it was a huge adjustment. I was fragile. I was emotional. I was still scared.

Ron and I weren't even speaking anymore. I can't explain the feeling I would get. I was free now, but so afraid of him and what he would do, I couldn't even speak to him. The divorce was a nightmare, but I knew it would be.

Chapter 12

This divorce was torment. There were days it seemed it just wasn't worth the pain, the money, or the stress. I questioned myself constantly. How could I stay with someone I knew didn't love me, and was that what I was supposed to do for my children? It was confusing. Other days I knew I was doing the right thing, I just couldn't live like that anymore, and I didn't want my children ending up the way I was living. What are the answers? How do you find the answers?

My parents had met when they were extremely young, married after a few weeks, and were married fifty-three years when my dad passed away. Why couldn't I do the same thing? What did they have, did they have that "lucky" thing I see in other couples? What was it?

Two failed marriages. I couldn't believe it, but I had to do it.

The struggle was never-ending.

Our every day life didn't really change much after I filed for divorce, because he was already living up in Fort Worth. He had lived away so much in the past, it didn't really feel any different in our home, not even slightly. I knew the girls would be fine, they would probably spend the same amount of time with him now, as before. I was sad when the girls left with him for visitation, but our lives were the same for the most part.

I tried to be friendly to Ron, especially in front of the girls, and had even told him when I filed for divorce, we should be friendly, for the girls. My first husband, Rachel's father, and I had developed a friendship after our divorce, and even spent time together with Rachel. It wasn't instantly, but we eventually became friends. He was always included in our important family functions. If Rachel had something special going on, he was always invited. If his mother was in town for a visit, I would take Hannah and Rachel to see her and she even treated Hannah like one of her own grandchildren. During the divorce from Ron now, when Hannah and Lizzie were with Ron for different holidays, I would spend time with Rachel and her dad. We would go to dinner or a movie.

This is what I thought was best for my children, for all of us. At one point, Hannah became a little jealous that Rachel had two fathers, and she only had one. When Lizzie came along, she also spent time with Rachel's dad on occasion, and told me she thought he was "awesome." This, I believe, is how we as divorced parents should behave, including the other parent in our child's life as much as possible.

It was something I had asked Ron to do from the beginning of our divorce, to remain friendly. He would not cooperate, and was cold from the beginning. I tried my best. One day when Ron was bringing the girls back to Corpus Christi at the end of one of his weekend visitations, he called me from the road. They were about an hour away, out in the middle of nothing, and had run out of gas. I jumped in my car, bought gas for him, and drove an hour to get the girls. I didn't even think twice, I just did what anyone would do. Isn't that what we are supposed to do?

For some reason I thought he would be nicer after this, friendlier, but no. I hated this behavior, because it wasn't good for the girls. I had thought that since we never lived together anyway, we could get divorced and at least be friendly in front of the girls.

A few months later, it was August, and Rachel was off to college. It was difficult to let go. I couldn't let go, completely. I just couldn't let go of my daughter. I tried telling myself this was not a choice, I had to find a way. Other people let their children go to college. This is normal, I would tell myself, over and over again. She was ready for college, and had been for a while.

She was out the door and ready to get her life going. I was happy for her. She was doing something I didn't do, she had graduated near the top of her class, and was now going off to a top university, to study Mechanical Engineering. I was proud of her. I was also having a really hard time letting her go, and was fighting it. It felt more like I was "losing" her, and not like she was merely going off to college. It felt like real loss. I felt so powerless, with Hannah and Lizzie now leaving with Ron so often, and now Rachel would be gone. It was painful. I was terrified.

We packed up both of our cars, and the day had finally arrived. My first child to leave for college. I had a knot in my stomach, and was completely filled with dread and fear.

It didn't help that she was going to be living on the thirteenth floor of a dorm building. Thirteenth. It filled me with even more fear. It hit me, I think, when we arrived at her dorm. She's going to be living here, and not at home. The moment I had been dreading, Rachel was at college.

This scared me to death. I panicked and started freaking out, telling her all sorts of things that could happen. I was annoying her. She asked me to leave once we got all of her things out of the cars and into her room. "But I was supposed to spend the night here," I told her.

"No," Rachel said, adamantly.

My mouth. My fear.

I found a coffee shop, got a large coffee, paid the girl, who was staring at me because I was sobbing. I couldn't help myself. I cried and cried the entire way home. It was eleven-thirty at night, and I was heading from Austin back to Corpus Christi, which is about a three hour drive. I called whoever I thought would be awake and willing to listen to me cry. Those poor souls. I was a mess. It felt like I had just lost my child. I did not handle it well, and my behavior was pitiful. Rachel did not call me for a couple of weeks, and looking back, it was probably for the best.

It was almost Labor Day, and we finally had something to be excited about, a wedding. Hannah, Lizzie and I were to join family in Portland, Oregon, for one of my nephew's wedding. We had never been there before, and the thought of going to a new place, and being with family, was very exciting. This was also the first time I had ever gone on a trip with my children, alone, and I was anxious to prove we could have the best time we'd ever had. That's exactly what we did. We had new clothes, stayed downtown Portland, took cabs everywhere we went, we were really "somewhere," doing wonderful things.

When we arrived downtown Portland, the girls and I walked around a few blocks, and found a few food trucks. We sat at the little tables around the trucks, eating our snacks, happy to realize we were there, so far from home. We sat for a while, people-watching and taking in the scenery around us. There were so many pretty things to see, the buildings, the trees, and it was a beautiful day. We walked around exploring until some of the family arrived. We went back to our hotel, which the girls absolutely loved, and got ready for the rehearsal dinner that evening.

After the rehearsal dinner, we all met up at a Starbucks in front of the main hotel where most of the family was staying, and we sat outside laughing and talking until really late. We took a cab back to our hotel, and as Hannah stepped out of the car, in her pretty new outfit, holding her Starbucks cup of hot chocolate, she said "I feel like I'm getting out of a limo in New York City." It was so sweet. She was so happy. She felt like we were really living the life! It warmed my heart. It was a little glimpse that the girls and I were going to be alright.

The wedding was beautiful, and Lizzie and some of her cousins shut down the dance floor late that night. They were having the time of their lives. They were all four or five years old. Lizzie enjoyed the conga line so much, she went around trying to get everyone to do it again, and one sweet lady joined her. It was a wonderful time. I was enjoying watching my girls have so much fun, especially since this was our first trip on our own.

During the day we joined my brother, his wife, and another couple that had been like family to us since I was a baby. We were going sight-seeing, just outside of Portland. First we drove to Multnomah Falls, about thirty minutes from Portland, along the Columbia River Highway. It was gorgeous. We walked up quite a few steps, about half-way to the top. We took photos, and simply admired the beautiful waterfall. My brother bought the girls ice cream, and then each a souvenir from the gift shop. They were truly having a great time.

We drove to the coast of Oregon, which was unlike any beach I had ever been to, including a couple of islands in the Caribbean, and multiple islands in Hawaii long ago, with Rachel's dad. There were giant rocks all along the beach. The beach, itself, was enormous and seemingly never-ending. I wasn't accustomed to walking so far to get to the water, from the car. In Texas, we park the car right on the beach, close to the water.

I had seen similar things in pictures, movies, but had never experienced anything like this before. The water was freezing, and we all took our shoes off and walked in the water. The girls had a lot of fun, even in the cold. They were extremely happy. We were happy. We enjoyed that trip more than I could have imagined.

Shortly after we got back home, to our reality, the girls went with Ron for a visit. When they came home, I noticed Hannah was acting strange. I couldn't figure it out, and it passed after a couple of days. I didn't think much about it, until it happened again, after the next visit. She was distant, and cold to me. Again, it would pass a couple of days later. Rachel would come home to visit, and she even noticed the difference in Hannah, so I knew it wasn't all in my mind. There was something happening, and I couldn't figure out what was going on.

The divorce was proceeding, moving along. After a couple of visits with Ron, Hannah was acting more out of character. I would try to talk to her, and ask her if something was wrong, but she would say she was fine. Suddenly, out of nowhere, I was told by my attorney that I needed to put Hannah in counseling, because she was depressed. Counseling? Depressed? What? We had just had that wonderful trip, and I knew she was extremely happy, now suddenly my daughter needs counseling for depression? I was really worried. There was something really strange going on. I had heard people say counseling worked for some people in our situation, but not others. I had a feeling this was not going to go well.

Her behavior was suddenly directed at me. It was

like a switch had been flipped. The next thing I knew, I was told that I was the source of her depression. I was starting to really panic. Nothing made any sense.

I took her to the first session with the counselor, and I explained to her what had been happening. I told her my concerns, that there was a change in her behavior, only after being with her father. I tried my best to make her understand what I was feeling, our history, I was hoping she understood. The fear inside of me was growing.

Hannah began coming home with all sorts of new things from her visits with her dad, including clothes, shoes, new laptop computer, and a new phone. Lizzie brought home nothing, but Hannah always had shopping bags full. Hannah would no longer hug me in front of her dad, or show any kind of affection towards me. She acted like she hated me, in front of him. She was still crawling into bed with Lizzie and I every night to watch a movie, but in front of him, she hated me. The next thing I knew, Hannah told me she was moving to Fort Worth to live with her dad, in a little over two months. What?

My world stopped.

Are you kidding?

No. Just no.

This was only the beginning.

I went overboard, trying everything to get her to stay. I was ridiculous. I catered to her every wish because I was so focused on losing her, and I became desperate. I was doing things that went against all of my beliefs on raising children, and spending too much money on her. I couldn't compete. I was losing, and I knew it. The more I knew it the worse my behavior became. I said things, terrible things, that upset her even more. I was fighting the fight, and losing.

I paid for a session with Hannah's counselor, begging her to help. I told her everything that was going on, and thought she could help Hannah see that she needed to stay with me. Please? I need help. Help us.

No, there was nothing she could do. It was explained to me that Hannah felt an unconditional love with me, but a very conditional love with her dad, and it was really hard to fight that kind of love.

What? Seriously? This is helping a child? Let her leave the parent she felt loved her unconditionally? What planet are we on?

I was feeling so defeated. I couldn't help myself, or my child. We were losing the fight. A fight that I thought everyone could see, but could do nothing to stop. Nothing.

People would say, oh, she's just a teenager, she'll be back. She's just a teenager, you know how teenagers are, this is just a phase.

This was no phase, and I knew it.

I was losing her, forever.

The mother of one of Hannah's friends came to pick Hannah up one day, and she actually told me, "You don't *seem* that bad." I don't *seem* that bad? What does that mean? I knew at that point either Ron, or Hannah must have told her I was "bad." If he thought I was "bad," why did he leave me alone all the time with the girls, while he lived away in Colorado, or at his mother's home in a different city all those years? If I was so bad, why did he cause the girls to run to their rooms and cry every time he came home to visit? It would happen every time he came home, because he would start changing our routine. I would always give them time after school to relax and have a snack. He would come home and take that time away from them, and insist they do their homework first. Homework can take hours, and they were used to having time and a snack first. They would begin to cry, out of frustration and exhaustion. We had a routine, and it worked. There was no reason for change.

How can I be so bad, that I can't be trusted with Hannah, but I could be trusted with Rachel and Lizzie? Why just Hannah? Didn't anyone else see anything wrong with this scenario?

I was panicked. Help! Someone help! I was terrified. I was asking everyone to do something, not knowing what could be done. It was excruciating, the thought of losing a child. Losing a child was my biggest fear. This was real fear. This wasn't just a case of a child choosing to live with one parent or another, and I knew it, I knew this was forever.

It was out of control. I was out of control. When you're the one losing a child, how are you supposed to act? My behavior was erratic, emotional, irrational. I didn't know any other way to act, my heart was being ripped out. When you're the irrational one, then everyone can look at your behavior and say, "oh, no wonder the child is moving, look at her mother's behavior." Funny how that well-oiled machine was working.

Weeks of out of control behavior, panic, terror, nothing changed. There wasn't anything I could do to change Hannah's mind, and not for any lack of trying. I was desperate, and the time had finally come.

The night before Hannah was to leave for Fort Worth, I begged her to stay. We sat, on the floor in her closet, crying. I was pleading with her, "please, stay, don't go, you have your friends here, family, a life here, Lizzie, and me. Don't leave us. I'll never get you back."

Nothing worked. I could see the little girl inside her eyes, but I couldn't reach her. She didn't want to hear me. Her excitement about moving to live with her dad was obvious, like she was going on some wonderful vacation. I couldn't compete. I lost. I told her if she was moving, then Lizzie and I would move to Fort Worth, also. I couldn't stand the thought of her living so far away, and I told her we would sell the house, and move as fast as we could. I couldn't bear the thought of him making my children fly back and forth on weekends. It wasn't the childhood my kids deserved. What have I done?

What have I done?

It was time for bed. She crawled into my king-sized bed with Lizzie and me, smelling like my Bath and Body Works lotion, and we put a movie on. The girls both fell asleep, and I cried. I couldn't sleep. There was a death happening, and I couldn't do anything to stop it. How unfair, I thought, even when you can see it's going to happen, you can't help at all, can't change a thing.

The next day, Ron showed up to get Hannah. She walked right out, got into the car, and they drove away. My heart was breaking, and he was enjoying it. My heart was in that car, driving away. Forever. He had wielded a sword, sliced me up, and left me there in a crumpled mess, and was enjoying every minute of it. He hit me where he knew he could hurt me the most, my Achilles heel . . . my child.

Loss. Pain.

No. Just no.

It felt like death. I was a wreck. I couldn't function. All I could think about was Hannah, and watching her drive away, leaving her life behind. My little Hannah, who loved family with all of her little heart. She had always been a thoughtful child, always thought of her family, and especially at Christmas. She loved Christmas.

When she was about six, maybe seven, as soon as our Christmas tree went up, usually in November, she would start her shopping. She would go around our home finding each of our "favorite" possessions, and wrap them up in secret. We would notice little gifts under the tree with our names on them. We would spend the next few weeks searching the house for our "favorite" possessions, only to realize they were the "gifts" under the tree.

As she got a little older, my parents would give all the kids twenty dollars, and take them to the dollar store. We had a big family, and for twenty dollars, you could buy everyone a gift. Hannah took it seriously, scanning the isles, searching for the perfect gift for her uncle, a cousin, her sister, until she found something for everyone.

She and Rachel fought a little when they were very young, but as they grew older, they didn't fight really at all. They loved each other. It made me so happy, because my own sister and I nearly killed each other. When Lizzie came along, Hannah was a little "mother" to her, she loved her baby sister with all of her heart. Hannah constantly drew pictures for her cousins, wrote sweet little notes to me and everyone else she cared about. She was such a thoughtful child. She even wrote me a little note of encouragement just before the birth of Lizzie, telling me that she knew I would do a "good job" having the baby. She always loved her family. She was taken from so many people that loved her, so many bonds were broken, stolen.

Watching her drive away, I knew down inside, this was going to be tough for her, some day. She was too young to see what she was doing, and she was ignoring anyone who was trying to warn her. Some of her best friends had tried to get her to stay, but nobody could get through to her, she would only listen to her father.

I told everyone I had to move, and move fast. I couldn't bear this separation from my child. I couldn't let Lizzie get on an airplane by herself, now only in kindergarten, and fly back and forth from Corpus Christi to Fort Worth every other weekend. Not happening.

People would say, oh, kids do it all the time, fly to see their parent, they'll be fine. I had already put them on a plane to go see him in Fort Worth, and that was not the way I wanted my children to remember their childhood.

There was a day that Ron was to bring the girls back from a visitation weekend, after Hannah had already moved to Fort Worth with him, he had Lizzie also, and showed up at my door. Hannah was to stay with me for a visitation. When they arrived, Lizzie ran straight inside the house, but Hannah wouldn't come in. She and Ron were standing there, on the front porch just outside the door, and Hannah began to cry. She didn't want to stay with me. She wanted to go to a friend's house. I couldn't understand where the drama was coming from, and asked her to come in for a few minutes. I even volunteered to drive her to her friend's house, if she would just stop crying, and come in for five minutes. Nothing worked. It was such strange behavior. I had never seen her act this way, cry like this, it was very odd.

I lost, of course, and he took Hannah over to the friend's, and I did not get my visitation with her. I was so shocked at the situation, and it hit me later that it seemed staged. It seemed as though it was a planned thing, and I thought about how he stood there looking down at his shoes, smiling, while Hannah cried tears. He was getting such satisfaction, joy even, from knowingly torturing me, and manipulating her.

There we were, planning to move, again. Again. Off to the unknown. Off to a place where we had no family, only a few friends here and there. I was afraid. Terrified. I was acting on pure emotion. My heart was completely broken.

I started getting my house ready to sell. I began searching for a place to live in the Dallas-Fort Worth area. I searched for a real estate office to work out of, and met a Realtor with one of the bigger companies. This was about the time the real estate market started to crash, and it was a little scarier knowing I wouldn't have any referrals to work on. I would have to start all over, from scratch. I would do my best. I had to do whatever it took to make it.

It took a while, but by the time everything came together, we had moved to the Fort Worth area. By this time I hadn't seen or heard from Hannah. There was no communication. It was constant rejection. She ignored my calls, ignored my text messages, ignored my emails. I kept thinking once I got up there, things would be different. I would get visitation time with her, and everything would be okay.

Ron had already reunited with an old girlfriend, and she was moving to live with Ron. They were getting married. Lizzie had told me that the new girlfriend had a daughter, and she was really sweet. I was actually excited, thinking Hannah, Lizzie, their future step-sister (almost Hannah's age), Rachel and I could all spend time together. I had visions of a house full of girls again, late night baking, movies, games. Talk about dreaming. I had no idea of the hell that awaited.

We lived about forty minutes away from where Hannah and her dad were living. I tried to reach out to her, but still nothing. It wasn't just me, it was her sister, Rachel, also, she wouldn't talk to her, either. It was beginning to seem as though she was taken from my side of the family.

Months went by. Ron remarried, his old girlfriend from years ago. Lizzie would go for visitation to his house, and come home talking about her new step-sister, and how much she loved her. I was happy Lizzie had someone to hang out with at his house, she spent a lot of time with her. She was sweet to Lizzie, and even though she was much older, she played with her and made Lizzie feel special. She would come home to me, and all she ever talked about was her new step-sister.

I was struggling to cope with no communication with Hannah. I had been asking everyone to help, to do something. Attorneys, friends, family, nobody could do anything, not even the judge, it seemed. It felt like I couldn't be heard, ever. Nothing worked. They didn't understand.

The pain. The loss. My child.

He always threatened to take my kids away, and look what he's done. He did it. He even got Hannah to sign a paper that said she wanted to live with him, through the court. It was over.

I was fighting to breathe, again. I was alone, and I did not want to live in North Texas, away from everyone and everything I loved. It never felt "right," from day one. It wasn't feeling like home, and made me feel even more lost.

I was walking out of the house to get into my car one day, soon after we moved, and suddenly a man walked up to me, and asked if I was Jennifer.

"Yes," I said, without hesitation.

He handed me an envelope, and told me I had been served papers.

What?

For what?

He left. The fear struck me immediately. I had a terrible feeling inside. I stood there and opened up the envelope. I could not believe my eyes. Near the top of the page was the word "custody."

Custody, of Lizzie. I froze. The world was falling in on me. I was being forced into a war, and I had no strength.

No. Just no.

Chapter 13

I was trying to get some sales going in real estate, but was having a hard time finding clients. The market was really down, and my head was a mess. My emotions were even worse. I showed some homes, but felt like I was just working for free. I took a different job, but it didn't work out, there was no organization in the company. I desperately needed structure, given the state I was in.

I bought a house in a different area of Fort Worth, for the school district. I wanted Lizzie to have a good life. It was a cute house, in a nice neighborhood. I tried to find the best possible place for her to live, and it was wonderful. The school was good, she made friends, learned how to ride her bicycle, and we were always outside doing something. Things were going well.

Lizzie began making friends a couple of days after we moved into our new house. One day when there were still boxes everywhere, I was just getting out of the shower, and I heard Lizzie screaming. "Mom, mom, there's kids climbing over the fence in the back yard, they are coming over to play!"

She walked into the bathroom and saw I was dripping wet from the shower, and yelled "Hurry, get dressed!"

I did as I was told, dressed as quickly as possible, and went outside to meet our new friends. There were two girls and a boy, all siblings. They became regular visitors, always climbing over our fence.

Shortly after our move, we were getting settled, and it began to snow. It snowed several inches, which didn't happen often in Texas. There was a thick layer of ice underneath, which made it dangerous to drive. We were snowed in. One day after being stuck at home in the snow, we heard lots of noise coming from around the corner, and decided to walk over and see what was going on.

We were slipping and sliding as we walked on the sidewalk, around the block. The noise became louder, and suddenly we saw at least a hundred or so people, all playing in the snow. There was a hill, and people had all kinds of sleds, boxes, even laundry baskets, and they were sliding down the hill. We couldn't believe we had moved to such a fun neighborhood!

We quickly began mingling, talking to people, some offering Lizzie a ride on their "sled." She rode down in a laundry basket a couple of times, and then one of the dads offered her a ride in their sled, which was actually the top part of a wheelbarrow. It was the fastest, the best of all the different sleds. She had a ball.

We went to straight to the store after the snow melted, and bought a little wheelbarrow, so we would be prepared for the next snow. We were beginning to feel adjusted, and I was relieved.

The custody lawsuit loomed overhead. I tried not to think about it, it was simply too much. Just the thought of losing Lizzie caused real pain.

My anxiety was getting worse, my sadness worse, and I tried doing a couple different jobs, but couldn't find the right atmosphere. I was functioning, but I was not a whole person. I would have little anxiety attacks and needed space to breathe. I couldn't handle anything that put pressure on me. A friend had recently become a

Massage Therapist, and I had read a few articles about it becoming more prevalent in medical care. The thought of not pushing paper in an office, and actually helping people, in a quiet space, sounded very appealing to me. I looked into it.

Soon I enrolled into yet another school, for Massage Therapy. I was excited, it was all new to me. Learning all the different bones, muscles, veins, the way the organs work, there was much more to massage than I ever dreamed. It was a nice change, different pace. It was just what I needed. A place of healing. I was going to help heal people, take their stress away. It was a good shift in my perspective.

The lawsuit dragged on and on. It was a few times in court, I'd have to testify, and he would have to testify.

I could only testify in the present, I couldn't talk about how I had raised the girls, mostly alone, for years. I took care of them, doctor's visits, dentist's visits, school, after school activities, fed them, did their laundry, took care of them when they were sick. I did it all. I wasn't perfect, but I did it, and I loved being a mother to my children. Unfortunately, I couldn't talk about the past, our history, only the present. Court is a nerve-racking experience, and it's not always fair. I was at the mercy of attorneys and a judge, neither of whom even knew me. These were total strangers, judging us and making life decisions for my children.

They didn't know our history. They didn't know I wasn't even myself anymore, I had been severely wounded, and wasn't whole. There was no way for them to know how much pain someone had caused other people. I took court, and being under oath seriously, and it is very discouraging to see other people lie in court. The fear of Ron taking Lizzie, after he had already managed to take Hannah, was always very real.

We were to have a court ordered "home study," someone appointed to come to our home and observe. I know this probably helps some children, but I always thought anyone can make things "look" a certain way. It really isn't the best measure of how good of a parent someone is, people can put on an act. It bothered me that a stranger would come and judge us, not knowing us, not knowing what we had already been through. I could have used a home study years ago, and we wouldn't be here in this lawsuit now, I thought. I had no idea how it all worked, I had no idea I would ever be in this situation.

All I ever wanted to be was a mother. How did I get here? It didn't seem possible. I had so much anxiety, when I would think about what was happening, pain would shoot through my head, right between my eyes, and all through my body.

Soon after, I got the text message. It was from her, Ron's wife. I had told her recently, that all I did was cry during our marriage, for over thirteen years.

"Did you really cry for over thirteen years?" she asked.

"Yes," I typed back quickly, "Why?"

And then, it began. Months of texting and talking, she was experiencing many of the things I had experienced in the past. Her marriage wasn't much different than mine had been, including her feeling that she and her daughter weren't important, and Hannah was the center of Ron's life. This did not surprise me at all, because Lizzie had mentioned a few things here and there after her weekend visits over at their house. I had just begun to date a man, and he was getting tired of the amount of time I spent trying to "help" this woman, after she had done nothing to help me with Hannah. We always thought she would finally realize something wasn't right, and try to reunite Hannah with me, and Rachel.

This was all too familiar to me, and I felt sorry for her. She told me all of the things he was saying about me, and I would immediately tell Rachel. We couldn't believe how stories had been twisted, to make me look abusive, and Rachel would be my helpless victim.

Rachel was angry, especially over one story his wife told me about a fight Rachel and I had over a cell phone. This fight occurred when Rachel was still in high school, living at home. The way she told the story, it sounded like Rachel was a helpless child trying to get away from her angry, abusive mother. The real story was that the mom was old, out of shape, and trying to wrestle the cell phone from a head-strong teenager to punish her, and lost, lost badly.

I'm not proud of that one day, one time I wrestled and physically fought with my child, but she was about to go off to college, still living in my home, breaking my rules. She was doing the things most teenagers do, dangerous things. Rachel was anything but helpless, she was an independent, strong-willed, hard-headed fighter, and a very smart girl. She was angry that Ron had been telling people his version of the fight, because she knew that *she* had been the clear winner that day!

I knew now, that fight was the weapon that was used to scare Hannah enough to leave me, and I couldn't believe it. Hannah had been standing there throughout that entire fight I had with Rachel. She even told me afterwards, that she couldn't believe how horrible Rachel was acting. She had seen it for herself, and now somehow she was playing along with the new, opposite version of the story. Now I knew. Now I could see what had happened to Hannah. The fear that was instilled in her, the gifts, it was all clear. My poor Hannah.

If I could, I would take that day back, in a heartbeat, if I could change the past.

Every time we went to court, nothing really happened, it was all a big waste of time and money, and caused more stress. There was nothing there, no big "shocker" that would allow him to take Lizzie away from me. Everyone knew what had happened, everyone told me he wouldn't get Lizzie. Lizzie was happy right where she was. The fear was always there, even though I knew better, I was still afraid, always. He had succeeded once, and would most likely keep trying, I knew he would keep trying until he had Lizzie.

Back when the case was beginning, I had just begun to date my boyfriend, Chris, and Lizzie liked him a lot. He was a spiritual, sweet soul. He waited on her hand and foot. She loved it. We all enjoyed hiking, and it became a ritual for us. We would try new places, new trails, but mostly just loved being outdoors, exploring. He loved to run, and Lizzie and I would follow on our bicycles, around our neighborhood, and the lakes that were up near the front entrance.

Chris took a job in Galveston temporarily, and we enjoyed going to the beach to visit often. We were always busy, and it seemed like things were good, but still no Hannah. She was always on my mind. Birthdays, holidays, we were being robbed of all kinds of possible memories. Every year that passed, I just couldn't believe so much time had gone by. It was difficult. The loss. I was grieving.

I couldn't look at a teenage girl that even remotely looked like her, without having an emotional reaction. It was difficult to hear other people say her name. Some people in my own family, and a few friends, would casually ask about her in conversation, and it hurt. I began to stop wanting to talk to these people, stop risking my feelings, stop letting myself get surprised. I'm sure they had no idea what was happening, I was in my own world. Some of them would just casually say things like, "Have you heard from her?" and I would instantly think to myself, if I had heard from her, the entire world would know! I'd be screaming it everywhere! Or, "Why don't you just go see her?" they would ask. As if I could just hop in the car, drive across Texas, and knock on her door, and have her welcome me into her arms. It hurt. They just didn't understand. The worst comment was that I should just "get over it." I was told to accept it and move on with my life. Move on.

Get over it? Move on?

If you saw a child being physically abused in front of you, would you simply get over it and move on? If you saw someone kidnap a child would you get over it and move on? No, I think most people would try to do something. Unfortunately, our situation was so foreign to everyone in our lives. This had never happened to anyone in our family, so there was no support. It wasn't until I found a book while browsing through Barnes and Noble, that I realized there was a name for what we were experiencing, Parental Alienation. There it was, a name for our pain and suffering.

When someone is rejecting you over and over, and you know in your heart they don't want anything to do with you, it's just not healthy to keep subjecting yourself to the pain. When the rejection is from your own child, a child you love unconditionally, the pain is truly unbearable. There was enough pain without more attempts at communication, to invite more rejection. Pain that never ended, and never became easier.

Even when I was sleeping, the dreams and

sometimes nightmares would haunt me. Dreams of Hannah when she was little, then older, sometimes happy, sometimes hurting and screaming for help. It was torment. I would awaken suddenly in the middle of the night and not be able to breathe, choking and gasping to get air. It was everything I could do to keep going, and try my best to be there one hundred percent for Rachel and Lizzie.

After years of battling, Ron finally dropped the case. His wife had left him. This did not come as any surprise. I hadn't seen or talked to Hannah in almost four years. The hole in my heart was causing me to sink deeper and deeper into sadness, depression. I could do the basics of life, but had to down-size my world quite a bit. I finished school, all of my classes and an internship, and passed the exam. I was now a Licensed Massage Therapist. I had reinvented myself, yet again. I would keep trying, keep going. My focus was Lizzie, and Rachel, and everything else had to come after them. They were the only people I had energy for.

I had become a completely different person.

I had moved to Fort Worth to be closer to Hannah, and to save the girls from all the travel. During the four years I had lived there, I never saw Hannah, not even once. Also during this time, my mother began to have more health problems, and it took over five hours to drive down to the ranch to help her. When Hannah graduated high school, and went off to college, there was no reason to stay there, in Fort Worth, there was nothing there for us. It was depressing. I was definitely in survival mode, I had fought as best I could, but always felt I had lost.

I enjoyed Massage Therapy, it was the first job I had ever had that made me feel I like I was really helping people. Clients would come in with different issues, stories, and a few times I would find myself caught up in their pain. One woman came in after just losing a small child. She was grieving, and telling me throughout the massage how much she was hurting. I tried not to become too emotional, but I couldn't stop my emotions. I felt like I was doing a really good thing, trying to take some of her pain away, while forgetting my own for an hour. It was the perfect job for me, I thought.

I was working, doing several massages a day, until I pulled some muscles in my arm. I lost the feeling in my hand, and had a lot of pain running up my forearm. I took some time off to heal, and tried everything to fix my arm. I couldn't do multiple massages a day anymore, it caused too much pain. I also couldn't play my piano, and I was getting really angry at life at this point. The world was out to get me. I just couldn't win.

My arm was not healing, even after a couple of weeks, and I was still in a lot of pain. I started having trouble with one of my hips, a recurring pain, from an old injury. I was a mess, again.

Now what? All that work, and now I can't do one single massage? Or play piano? Or feel my hand?

I felt like I wasn't living, it felt like I was just learning how to lose people, lose things, I was losing everything. I was trying to learn how to accept loss, and I wish I could say I did this gracefully, but I certainly did not. My fear, my pain, my bitterness and anger, were all building inside of me. I couldn't cope with any conflict. I was spinning out of control, and my anxiety only grew. It was beginning to seriously affect my health. I was feeling ill almost every day, all day.

Is this all I'm ever going to experience? Loss? It was difficult enough to get through school in the shape I was in, only half a person, and now I am left with nothing, again?

All of my fear was targeted at the world, all my anger at people. I truly thought everyone was betraying me, lying to me, talking about me. Nobody was helping get Hannah back. One of my brother's was even hanging around Ron, which I felt was the most horrible betrayal of all. It seemed like everyone had accepted my loss and gotten over it, everyone but me, Rachel, and Lizzie. The three of us were still suffering. I knew Hannah was suffering as well, in her own world, her world that I knew absolutely nothing about. I didn't know how she felt, but I knew we missed her, and we were in pain because of her loss.

My anger and fear always came straight out of my mouth, disguised as hurtful words, aimed at whoever I thought was "attacking" me. I couldn't help myself anymore.

I was clawing and scratching my way through almost every close relationship I had, whether they were family, or friends, I could never really trust anyone, not even a little bit.

I became defensive, convinced at this point that the world was trying to make me suffer. I became so angry at anyone that wasn't helping me get Hannah back, even if it wasn't rational. I became angry at the people I was closest to, because they didn't seem to understand, or feel the severity of what had happened. They weren't feeling what I was feeling.

I had tried to get myself in a good place, I even told myself many times that my daughter was alive, and I should be thankful, because so many children die. I was grateful, I knew my child was alive. I am not comparing our situation or grief to that of those who have lost a child to death, there is no question, that has got to be the worst pain in the world.

I simply wanted my daughter back. It was a different kind of grief than I had ever experienced. The grief never ended, never got easier. I didn't get to go through all the normal steps of grief. I was stuck, always, at the beginning. The beginning of shock, disbelief, pain, the feeling of helplessness. It had been years. Years of trying to stay hopeful, years of trying to live with the torment.

Years of wondering how in the world someone can take a child because of bitterness and revenge, and get away with it. A child is not a possession. How can someone do this and not be punished? How can one person cause so much pain for so many people, and still stroll through life unscathed?

I was angry.

Chapter 14

We moved. I was running away from the grief. We moved to Houston. We had family there, including my dad's only sibling, my aunt, and plenty of friends. Ron's family was there. I was raised there. I thought we could move there and start over. I loved knowing we were close to the beach again, it was a little under two hours away.

Unfortunately, we did not enjoy our life there. I was drowning, and Lizzie wasn't as happy there. It didn't feel right. Lizzie wasn't enjoying school, and didn't really fit in. I felt awful because Lizzie had always enjoyed school before. We had been so excited for this move, but we didn't feel comfortable.

One day Lizzie and I were out riding our bicycles. We had just started out on our usual ride through our neighborhood, and my cell phone rang. It was Rachel. She was crying, and I could barely understand what she was saying. One of my eldest brother's sons, my nephew Daniel, had suddenly died.

No. Please no. Not again.

He was twenty-nine.

It didn't seem real, at first. I hadn't seen him in a while, maybe two years, because he was living on the other side of Texas. I wasn't close to anyone in that part of the family anymore, and I had completely shut them out.

My nephew, besides my sister and I, was the only other adopted child in the entire family. When they first adopted him, I was nineteen. He was a special child. He could talk like an adult when he was only eighteen months old. Literally. He was exceptionally bright. I spent a great deal of time with him, I wanted him to be mine. I even took him on dates with my first husband, before we were married, so he could spend time around a baby. I was crazy about Daniel. We had always been close, always.

When he was about fifteen, he and I went to see the movie Titanic together, and just before the movie started, he pulled a little stack of tissues from his pocket and handed them to me. "Here, Jen, I know you're going to need these," he said in a sweet, thoughtful way. When I had divorced Ron and had to let Hannah and Lizzie go with him for the first Christmas, I was very emotional and lonely. During that time, Daniel had planned to get his first tattoo, along with his dad and brother. When his dad and brother chickened out, I decided to go with him and get my first tattoo, my first and only tattoo. It was meaningful and a very special experience because of him. He was gone? It wasn't sinking in at all. How could he be gone? How could this happen to our family . . . again?

I wanted to help, wanted to do something, but I hadn't spoken with any of them in so long, and there were bad feelings. I knew I had to do the right thing, and help. That's what you're supposed to do in this situation. There would be a funeral service in the same place where we had held a service for my dad. He would be buried next to my dad, and a reception afterwards, at my mom's house.

A niece in Houston, my other brother's daughter, and I were going to take all the food and supplies. We organized the plan, and put it into motion. It was really scary for me, seeing this part of the family. I was angry they hadn't helped with my situation with Hannah, angry about so many things. I didn't know if I was even welcome, but I had to be there. There wasn't a doubt. It's the right thing to do.

We showed up early, unloaded our cars, and began to get dressed at my mom's. We got back in the car to drive to town for the service. It was sad. Everyone was there. Daniel's ex-wife and little girl were there. His daughter was young, maybe six years old. As we all sat and watched a video of photos showing his entire life, I was struck by his appearance. I barely recognized him in the more recent photos. It made me very sad, that I hadn't seen him in the last couple of years of his life. I whispered to one of my other nephews sitting next to me, "Is that what he looked like?" I couldn't get over the change. He was thin, and his eyes looked sad. It was a shock. I wished I had been able to see him one more time, but now he was gone.

I went down the line after the service, and hugged his immediate family, my brother and his family, told them how sorry I was. I truly was sorry. I loved him. I loved all of them. I just couldn't be close to them anymore. I skipped the burial to get back to work at the house for the reception. I left Lizzie with Rachel, and some of the family. I stayed focused on getting everything laid out on tables, and ready for when the guests started to arrive.

I was as polite and tried to be as helpful as I had ever been, trying so hard to do the right thing. Most of all, I was trying to keep my own feelings and anger deep down inside. As I was standing at the large coffee pot, the percolator kind that makes forty cups of coffee, and laying out sugar and creamer, one of my brother's walks up to get coffee. I hadn't seen him in a few years, and didn't want to, because I knew he was friendly with Ron.

I was told by my niece, that my brother had actually agreed with Ron, that he was right in taking

Hannah from me. I'm sure he was told the story of Rachel and I fighting over the phone, and after hearing this, I guess he was convinced. It was infuriating, and extremely hurtful. This particular brother had divorced his first wife when his children were very young, and had never really raised his own kids. How could he possibly know what I was going through? How could he possibly judge me as a mother, without ever knowing what it took to actually raise a child? I had done it for years on my own, and my girls were all good kids. He, himself, had actually told me I had raised the best children in our entire family. How could he betray me, without even talking to me instead of Ron? It really bothered me, the unfairness, the judgment. It hurt.

"What's Ron up to, where's he working?" he asked. It was all he said to me that entire day.

I was stunned. What? Really? That's the only thing you have to say to me? I knew he had talked to Ron. I knew he had even met up with him in California for a college football game, and Hannah was there. He had even sent word to me, he wanted me to know Hannah was getting close to calling me, and I should be ready, but I shouldn't be emotional if she calls.

What? I haven't seen or talked to my daughter in years, and I'm not supposed to be emotional if she calls? There was to be no more communication between this brother and I, never, there was too much betrayal, too much pain. He didn't bother to talk to me about the situation with Hannah, and was completely insensitive towards my suffering, and the suffering of all of my girls. I couldn't even look at him anymore. It was painful.

I didn't even talk to him. I just walked away. I tried to remain busy, just get through, get through this awful day. It was getting more difficult to keep my feelings of hurt and anger inside.

My other brother, Daniel's father, walked up to me after a while and told me he was glad I came to the funeral, and I had done the right thing. I told him there was no doubt in my mind I needed to be here, no question. I loved Daniel very much. I didn't even think of not coming. He told me I was a good girl. That was all he said to me. I did the right thing. His words were hanging in my head, and I became even more angry, and hurt. I am a good girl.

A good girl. I was in my late forties at this time, and this was actually insulting to hear. I knew my brother and his family were hurting, I knew they were still in shock and pain. I hurt for them. I was in pain. I was still in pain because none of them had done the right thing for me, when Hannah was taken from me, right before their eyes. They hadn't helped me when I was begging for help. I was trying not to be selfish, but I was so shocked at their behavior. It was feeling like I was the only one ever doing the right thing. I was the good girl.

I was so angry, and hurt, by the whole experience. This was my world. Anger, hurt, betrayal, and so much loss, it was all negative. No matter how hard I was trying, I could not get past myself, my own pain, my own feelings. I would feel guilty, but justify my anger with their behavior. So much anger. So much hurt.

I stayed to the end, until the day was done, and everything was cleaned up and packed away, and everyone was leaving. Lizzie and I went home. I still couldn't even believe Daniel was gone. It still didn't seem real. I couldn't accept his death, not yet.

My mom was not handling losing another grandchild, another huge loss for her, for our family. I realized we had made a huge mistake moving to Houston.

I knew my dad would want us to be closer to my mom.

We moved to Austin. Yes, I said moved to Austin, to be closer to Rachel, my mom, my sister, simply to be near this part of our family again. I wanted Lizzie and Rachel to be close. They loved each other so much, and I felt they needed to spend more time together, especially since we had just suffered another loss. It was important, crucial for my girls.

Rachel had finally graduated and was working as an engineer. My mom was only an hour away, we would get to see her more. As soon as we moved, I was served papers, again.

I knew it was coming, but we couldn't sit up there in Fort Worth now that Hannah wasn't even there, and the move to Houston was simply a mistake. I had to hire another attorney, and go through another lawsuit. Lizzie was eleven.

The day I had been dreading, the day we were to be in court, finally arrived. We made the drive to Dallas, all of our tensions were high. Ron brought yet another new wife, who had apparently been another old girlfriend. I noticed there was a third person, a young woman. I glanced quickly at her, and there was something very familiar about her. It took a couple of seconds to register, but I suddenly realized it was Hannah.

Hannah. It was Hannah.

It didn't really sink in at first. There she was. I hadn't seen her in person in years, and she was all grown up. Twenty. Her face had changed, her hair had changed, she wasn't the little girl I remembered. I had seen a few pictures of her over the previous years, but nothing prepared me for seeing her in person. It truly was like seeing a ghost.

It only lasted for a few minutes, and she was gone

again, but we would be coming back to court another day. I wanted so badly to try to talk to her, but after years of rejection, all the texts, phone calls, cards, emails, she ignored all of it for years. I wanted to scream. I wanted to grab her and hug her. I couldn't take any more rejection, and I knew she couldn't talk to me in front of her father.

We left, quickly. Chris, Lizzie and I drove back to Austin. It had been difficult, traumatic even, so traumatic I literally passed out on the way home. I wished I had known she would be there, I would have been able to prepare myself. I wondered what Hannah must have felt, seeing me for the first time in years. Was she feeling the same things I was feeling? I would never know. It was so unfair.

The next time in court, we all had to testify, one by one, Ron, me, Rachel, and Hannah. I didn't know what the purpose of all of this was, we always had to try to roll with whatever Ron wanted. I sat in the court room, Hannah was a few feet in front of me, on the witness stand testifying, against me. I felt like I was being treated like a criminal, and couldn't help but be angry that my children had to testify.

As I stared at her, I tried to listen, but memories kept flooding in, Hannah as a baby, a toddler, then kindergarten, etc. All the times she did something really funny, or sweet, my mind was overloading. I just kept looking at her. I couldn't stop looking at her. After years of not hearing her voice, seeing her face, she was sitting ten feet in front of me. I was closely studying her mannerisms, the way she spoke. I was trying to connect the little girl I knew to the young adult now sitting in front of me. It was surreal. This child, my child, she was all grown up, and I missed it. Her voice was the same, but it didn't match her face, her pretty, young adult face. The things she was saying didn't make sense, it was all old information, from years ago.

This was all the information she was supposed to talk about during the last lawsuit for custody of Lizzie, a few years before. Ron's last wife had told me how he would sit with Hannah, and talk about the case, something we were never supposed to do. How sad for her, I was just hurting for her. She had no idea that these things she was saying were not making any sense. She was doing what she thought she was supposed to do, I thought. I left the courthouse that day feeling so sorry for her, feeling guilty I hadn't realized what was happening in time to stop it. This girl had been kept from many people who love her. It wasn't right to do that to a child.

All I could see was that little girl who I sat in the closet with the night before she left, that look in her eyes, she was doing what she thought she was supposed to do. Not what was in her heart. I remembered how I felt when my father had asked me to move into the apartment with my sister, with tears in his eyes, and I felt the need to help him, be who he wanted me to be. This was happening to my own daughter, and I understood.

I realized Hannah and I had something similar in our life-journeys, we were both put in a position to please our fathers, and make a decision that would change our lives forever. Although different decisions, and different consequences, we were both so young to have made such enormous decisions that would impact our lives. It was so difficult to think of my child, my daughter, and what the impact of these last few years were going to have on her as a woman. I know the things that happened to me living outside my parents home as a teenager impacted my entire life, my soul, my personality, my perspective on the world. I wanted to talk to Hannah, I wanted to know how she was doing, I wanted to help her. It was painful.

I thought about the time she kicked me, as a toddler, because she couldn't show anger towards her dad. At that moment something inside of me just knew, she had been fighting another battle her entire life. I had been oblivious to her struggle. It was my responsibility as her mother to protect her, and I had failed. I missed all of the subtle clues, the obvious clues, she had been controlled since she was a toddler. I had been controlled, and was still being controlled by the fear, fear of my children being taken away. We were being controlled by fear. Not love. Never love.

Just being taken to court for custody is enough to make anyone doubt themselves, it's a tough thing to go through. When you know there isn't anything about you that is so questionable that a judge would take your kids, you still find yourself questioning every decision you've ever made. You still question everything about yourself.

Even if I had been this horrible mother, the person Ron told everyone I was, why did other people have to suffer? Why did Rachel have to suffer? Why couldn't she have a relationship with her sister, even if I was so terrible? Lizzie? Why weren't Hannah and Lizzie close now? My mother, Hannah's grandmother? What did they all do?

Nothing. Nobody did anything. She was just taken away. Stolen. Just like he said he would do if I ever divorced him.

We settled everything in court, it didn't take long. Nothing changed, except maybe the child support, it had a way of decreasing with every court visit. No change in anything having to do with custody, and I didn't care about the rest. My little Lizzie and I were going to be fine.

When we were leaving the court, I watched

Hannah turn and walk away with her dad, and his wife. It killed me. I wanted so badly to talk to her, to hug her. I knew I couldn't, she couldn't, but I was aching inside. This might be the last time I ever see her, I thought, the last time I ever see my daughter.

It was brutally painful, to have her dangled in front of me, the child I had been grieving for so many years. To see her and not get to hug her, or talk to her, or tell her I miss her and love her with all of my heart, was cruel. I wanted to grab her and tell her how sorry I was for everything she's been through, but it wouldn't happen. It wasn't possible. It was tough to accept, but I had no choice. The wound was reopened, and I now had to try my best to heal again, which usually meant trying to stuff it all down inside, and act as normal as possible.

Lizzie and I could begin our life in Austin, and we were loving it. We felt so much better there, like we could breathe. We were quickly out doing things, hiking throughout the hill country, driving to the little country towns all around us, we were loving our new surroundings. Lizzie was enjoying school, she was making friends, and loving being in band for the first time. We were seeing Rachel more, and visited my mom a few times out at the ranch.

Things were finally feeling a little more normal. Chris had been telling me about his favorite church in Austin, for years. One Sunday, finally, we made the drive across town to this church. I immediately felt some kind of connection with the pastor. He was so real, so humble. He was enthusiastic but not over-bearing. He spoke in a way that was easy to listen to, and easy to understand.

This was the first time church had ever felt comfortable for me. I bought my very first Bible. I would read a little, and enjoy church, and felt good when I was there, but it still just didn't help me with any of my struggles, my pain, my grief. Chris and I both would get very emotional at church, but the minute we walked out the doors, it was back to reality.

We were beginning our new life in Austin, and I had systematically separated myself from most of my family, and was pulling back from a few friends. I was still down-sizing. Where once I would be on the phone every day with a different friend, or family member, now I only spoke to a handful of people, and sometimes days in between conversations. It was all about Rachel, Lizzie, and trying to build a new life. I kept in contact with my mom, and my sister, but not nearly as much as I used to, I was secluding myself. I still had a lot of anger inside, and was still grieving. I was trying to heal, trying to be better, but I was still a mess. Seeing Hannah at court, having all of that pain brought to the surface again, it was taking my depression to another new level.

My arm wasn't healing, and the feeling in my fingers was still gone. It upset me that I had made this life-changing decision to become a Massage Therapist, and I was unable to massage. I couldn't play piano like I could before, and it was really hard for me to accept. It was always the time I felt really relaxed, the hour or two at night after Lizzie went to bed, when I could sit and play. It was the only time I could get the world and all of my troubles out of my mind.

Chris got a job in health care, and he said they had an opening for someone in the activities department at his place of work. He said it involved entertaining a group of seniors with Dementia, Alzheimer's, Parkinson's Disease, and that I would love it. It sounded good to me, and I went to interview, and got the job.

I felt overwhelmed very quickly, it was so sad to

see people so helpless. It was difficult to see how their memories had been stolen from them, their brains taken over, and their families devastated. I'm not sure it was the best atmosphere for me to be working in every day, given my circumstances, given the state of grief I was living in. I was not a whole, healthy person, by any means.

I began to fall in love with a few of the elderly residents, and enjoyed learning about them. They could remember things from their lives in detail, but nothing from two minutes ago, or sometimes even thirty seconds ago. It was difficult to adjust, to remember their short-term memory simply wasn't there anymore. I did my best, considering.

One little lady in particular, stole my heart. She was such a delight. She had so much dignity, and a wonderful sense of humor. I fell in love with this ninety-five year old woman! She would get horrible anxiety frequently. She had dementia, and I learned to reach over and hold her hand while we were all playing a game, or doing some other activity, and she would be better. She called me her best friend. She melted my heart.

As I was setting up tables for an activity one day, she was sitting close to me, watching as I worked. I had to get all of these different "props" out for different activities. If it was a tea party, there were tea sets, books about teas, little signs, different decorations for every activity. I was putting things out on the table in front of her. Suddenly, she says "Your aunt wants you to move that thing over to there," and she pointed where I was supposed to put it. I moved the object, and then realized maybe my aunt was here in spirit. She had just died suddenly about a year before. I asked, "My aunt?" All she said was "Yes."

That day I met three different women at work, one

lived there, and the other two were visiting family. All three had another one of my deceased aunt's name, her first and middle names. Three different women. I knew after the third, it was another aunt with me that day, one who had died when I was about ten years old. I couldn't believe this was happening. I had been watching a show called *The Long Island Medium* for years, hoping I'd be lucky enough to get some type of message from one of my "spirits," and now I had my aunt with me. Forty years after she passed away. And what a bonus, I now had my very own little Texas "Medium!"

One day when we were all listening to live music up at the front, my friend, my Medium, started having anxiety. She was beginning to call out, yell to people from her past. I decided to take her back to her section of the building, so she didn't bother anyone listening to the music, and also so she would feel more comfortable.

I was pushing her in her wheelchair, while holding her hand, and I was leaning forward over her, pushing mostly with my body. I had my head down really close to her, and was talking to her as we made our way all the way around to the very back of the building. We were in a long, empty hallway, and she suddenly says "Your husband, John, sure is a good dancer."

"My husband? You mean my dad?" I quickly asked. I knew immediately what was happening.

"Oh, yes, your dad, he loves to dance."

"Yes, he does." I knew my dad was talking to her. I knew it. How in the world would she know his name, or that he loved to dance? He's here! Oh my gosh, he's here!

"He says you're a wonderful daughter, and he is just so proud of you!"

I couldn't speak, except to say thank you. It was incredible, and filled me with love.

Chapter 15

In my heart I knew this job was not the right job for me. I knew I was not really strong enough to go through the process of losing the people I was "entertaining" every day. To be honest, I wasn't even strong enough to get through one day. I already felt worn down after a few short weeks. I had a feeling I wasn't going to last there for long. There were a few conflicts with the schedule. I worked late, and I had to take my lunch break late in the afternoon, and use that time to go pick up Lizzie from school, and drive all the way back to work. It used up the entire hour. I felt fortunate that I could bring her to work with me, but it was draining. Lizzie and I would get home so late at night, completely exhausted, with no time or energy for anything else. It was not a good fit.

I wasn't eating right, I was not getting enough sleep, and it was wearing on me. The emotions I was having every day at work were overwhelming. I was not a whole person, and could feel myself really slipping downward. It was beginning to affect my relationship with Chris even more. Although I loved watching Lizzie and the seniors interacting with each other, I thought it was good for all of them, the job didn't last.

I wasn't strong enough for that atmosphere, not whole enough. I missed all of the seniors, but didn't miss the place. I think I was there simply to learn, and have my encounters with my aunt, and especially my dad. I missed my dad, and had fantasized so many times about getting a "message" from him, or hearing from his spirit in some way, and it had happened. I felt in my heart that's why I was there in the first place.

Chris sent me a text message the night my little lady friend passed away, he was there at work when it happened. He had been telling me she wasn't doing well, and we knew it was coming. He simply wrote, "She's home." I cried and cried. I was happy for her, she would be with her family now, her husband, and the daughter she had lost. I still cried. I felt such a loss. I had only known her for a few short months, but I loved her.

After this, I decided to start my own massage business. From everything I had learned lately, it was probably best that I controlled my own work schedule. I wanted so desperately to do massage, and was determined to do it even if my arm wasn't healed. I did research and planned everything out. I ordered my business cards, bought a new set of scrubs, and wrote out and printed a little bit of literature describing my business. I knew exactly where to find my clients. I was ready to go, even with a bad arm.

About this time, I received an invitation in the mail for an anniversary celebration for some friends of mine. I had known them since before I had Rachel, now twenty-six. They had been married forty years, and their three daughters were giving them a party. I felt like I needed to go, I had turned down so many invitations over the last few years, secluding myself from everyone, but I felt like I needed to do this. They were one of my favorite families, and it was important to join them for such a special occasion.

It took everything I had to make myself go, many times I thought I'd call and give my regrets, but I held on.

I had become very selective about social situations I let myself get into, because I knew I wasn't whole. I wasn't healthy, emotionally, and was extremely depressed. My wounds were always fresh, stuck in the beginning of the grief cycle over Hannah. It was always there, that vulnerability, that fragile feeling I felt around other people. It was especially difficult to be around people with daughters, or close-knit families, which were constant reminders of my loss. I didn't feel comfortable at all around people that had known the "old" me, because I felt I was so changed at this point, and had to pretend to be happy. I would feel very insecure, knowing I wasn't a good actor, and trying to hide the shame of my failures.

I was proud of myself for taking the risk, and drove to Dallas. I arrived at the hotel and had plenty of time to get dressed. I tried to stay positive, and focused. Chris was supportive, and had talked to me on the phone for much of the drive. When I was all ready to head over to the party, he asked me to text him a picture of myself, because I rarely got this dressed up anymore. He told me to try to have a good time, and to call him after the party.

I was nervous, but was feeling fairly confident I could do this. I drove to the restaurant, nerves and all, and joined the dinner. It was one of my favorite Italian restaurants, with a warm atmosphere. The hostess directed me to the private room towards the back of the building. As I walked down the hallway, passing other private rooms, my nerves were getting the best of me. I tried to calm down, and took a couple of deep breaths before I opened the door and walked in the room.

One of their daughters was speaking when I walked in, and another motioned to me to join her at her table. There were six or seven tables of people, and I was sitting with two of the daughters, and their children. I had known these girls since they were children, and now to see them all grown up, all mothers with children of their own, was heart-warming. Before I had Rachel, I would have the girls over for popcorn and movies. They were all such good girls, such sweet kids, and spending time with them made my desire to be a mother even greater.

I was enjoying the evening, sipping wine and reminiscing. I was beginning to relax a little bit. After dinner was over, one of the girls walked up and set a white envelope on the table in front of me. I reached down and opened it without thinking, and there was a photograph inside. I held it up to look at it, and saw that it was an old picture of myself, and my sweet little Hannah sitting on my lap. I froze. I looked closer. She looked to be about two or three years old. This photo was taken at their home when we had gone for a visit, eighteen or nineteen years before. I stared at her face. I started to tear up. I was crumbling. The feelings I had stuffed way down inside were fighting their way out. Suddenly I remembered my pain, and how I had failed my children. Sitting there with this wonderful family, and surrounded by all of this obvious, lasting love in the room, I felt inferior. The facade I had built up around myself for the evening was shattering.

I excused myself and went to the restroom. I tried to get over it quickly. It had taken me by surprise. A picture of my own child. I couldn't handle anything anymore, not even this simple little gesture, which was sweet on their part. I was just a mess.

I made it back to my hotel, called Chris, and cried. I held the picture of me and Hannah, staring at her little sweet face and cried more.

As I drove back home the next day, I just kept thinking that this was exactly the reason I can't attend these kinds events, I'm not strong enough to be in public. Back to seclusion, it's safer.

Shortly after this, just as the school year was beginning, my little Lizzie was diagnosed with severe Scoliosis. Shock. We were in shock. Lizzie and I sat looking at the X-ray on the screen while the doctor explained what was wrong. Severe curvature of the spine, Scoliosis. Severe starts at forty, or forty-five degrees, and the curve of her spine was at seventy.

Seventy? I was zoning in and out. I was trying to focus on his words, but it was not making any sense. How is this happening?

She's at the right age, twelve, having a growth spurt, it just happens, he told us. Idiopathic Scoliosis, which means they don't know exactly why it happens. We listened as he explained a surgery that he suggested, because there really were no other options. No other options. Surgery. My mind was reeling.

No other options. Major surgery. They would be placing metal into her spine, I couldn't even hear him anymore. We were sitting there, stunned.

Lizzie was holding my hand so very tightly. She was scared. I could see it on my girl's face.

We left his office with some literature, an order for an MRI and CT scan, in pure disbelief.

No. Just no.

What? How can this be happening to my girl? My Lizzie was such a good girl, so good I actually had to tell her to break a rule once in a while. This child who always does the right thing, treats everyone the same, just good. She was twelve years old, so young to go through this. My older two girls had never gone through anything other than a few stitches, the flu, nothing even close to this. This was Lizzie's second surgery. Almost two years before she had to have a small foot surgery. Nothing this intense, but now her second surgery.

I tried to be as positive as possible.

She kept looking at me, and asking how this could be happening to her, why, why mom?

We came home exhausted that day, put our pajamas on, and laid on the bed holding hands, in complete shock. Chris was shocked, as well, but was strong for Lizzie. He kept assuring me she would be fine, she would be fine. Stay positive.

Stay positive. The goal.

Me, staying positive? This was going to be a challenge, to say the least.

We could do this. Other families get much worse news, and I said we were grateful our situation could be fixed with surgery. Grateful. Stay grateful.

On the surface, I was trying so hard to be strong, positive, but down deep inside I was panicked. There was so much fear.

There were so many risks, operating so close to her spinal cord, risks that went through my head constantly. It was starting to feel like death. There was a darkness inside of me I couldn't shake. My thoughts went to a very low place, especially at night when I would lie down to sleep. The fear was overwhelming. Could this be it? Could I be losing another child? Is God angry at me, and this is my punishment? With the loss of Hannah, and my greatest fear being to lose a child, I thought God was somehow trying to show me what *really* losing a child means. This thought consumed my confused and fearful mind. I actually thought many times that whatever you fear the most will most likely happen. I was already weak, and not whole, before we even received this diagnosis, this was beginning to put me over the edge already. I did my best to keep it all down inside.

It was tough. I begged God to help my girl. Help her, take her fear away. The same God I thought was punishing me. I was completely confused about God, and frankly, I was doubting everything at that point. I didn't think I was going to make it through this, but wanted to be strong for Lizzie.

We didn't tell very many people at first, kept it all to ourselves for a little while, I couldn't even talk about it. There was some denial, still some shock. Lizzie would tell her friends at band camp, but come home and still not even believe it herself. She would still look at me and say "why mom, why me?" We would always come to the conclusion that we should be grateful it wasn't something more horrible. Maybe she was going to do something wonderful in her future because of this awful experience. Grateful, stay grateful.

The first thing we had to do was to pick a date for the surgery. We wanted to have it as soon as possible. She didn't want to miss band, and knew she wouldn't be there for their seventh grade regional competition. She knew they would have to replace her in one of the bands she was in. We were still trying to deal with the impact this would have on her life, but thought the sooner we get it over with, the better.

The doctor's office called me a few days later to schedule surgery, and it was done, six weeks from that day. Six weeks. Six weeks seemed like tomorrow and forever at the same time. We just wanted this nightmare to go away.

There was so much to plan, so much to do. We would have to get on Home Bound Services for school. A teacher would come to our house twice a week, for two hours each time. She would help Lizzie keep up with school work. I filled out all the paperwork, had a meeting at the school, and it was set up.

Driving to get the MRI, I was still questioning everything in my head, why her, why can't it be me, I've never had an MRI, I have been so lucky. Why her? I didn't know what to expect.

We arrived at the radiology center, went in, took a seat to fill out the paperwork, and wait. We sat there for about half an hour, and I was looking at all the babies there. How sad, I thought, babies, there for some test because they have some dreaded disease, or problem. It was all so heartbreaking. Lizzie and I talked quietly, surrounded by people, families.

We had been sitting there for a while, and I looked down at the floor in front of us. Right in front of us. I knew I had looked there before, but hadn't seen it, a penny. There was a little shiny penny on the floor. I had always heard that spirit leaves pennies for you. I always thought the old song "Pennies from Heaven" was talking about this very thing. I reached down to pick it up, and told Lizzie that I thought maybe my dad, her Pappaw, whom she had never met, was with us. I hoped this was a sign that everything was going to be alright. Everything *had* to be alright.

She believed it as well, and she said she had been finding pennies all of the sudden, everywhere she went. This gave us a little peace, a little comfort. We would be fine, I told myself, trying so hard to believe.

She was a little scared of the unknown, but Lizzie was so brave, my girl was handling whatever she faced with so much courage. They finally called our name, and took us back to another area. They told Lizzie she would have to lay perfectly still for three tests, all taking about twenty-five minutes or so, each. I would sit just outside the room, and wait. As I sat waiting in the little side area, I could hear an extremely loud noise coming from the room around the corner. Shortly after it stopped, about an hour later, Lizzie came walking up to me. The technician was right behind her, "She's all done," she said. It was over. She did it.

On the way home she described what it was like, how she had laid on the table, wearing earphones, but the machine was so loud she could barely hear the music. She was relieved it was over. One tiny step in our journey was done.

Next the CT scan, at a different place, different day. We showed up early, and they got us in and out quickly. It wasn't as involved as the MRI. Done.

On the way home Lizzie was telling me about her experience once again, and was laughing because they would always tell her "You did so good!" As if you have a choice. This test was actually interesting, this would be the actual "picture" they use on a computer screen during surgery. We tried to stay positive.

After all the tests, now we only had the "pre-op" visit to the hospital, during which they would show us exactly where she would be during all stages of the surgery. The hospital was awesome, a large children's hospital in Austin. It was a beautiful place, with all kinds of art and beautiful architecture. Everyone there was very sweet to Lizzie, they all seemed to enjoy their jobs, and were so comforting to her. The last place anyone wants to be is in a hospital, having major surgery, but the atmosphere was so pleasant, we already felt fortunate to be there.

Lizzie had to have her blood drawn, for the first time. They couldn't find her veins. You couldn't see even one tiny vein on either of her arms. Another obstacle.

They tried a few different methods, but nothing worked. Finally, a woman walked in the room, looked at Lizzie's arms, and somehow saw a vein that none of us could see. Like magic, she drew her blood. It was truly unbelievable, and the other nurses said she simply has "the touch." She truly has a gift. Lizzie made it through, and we were now set for surgery. A couple of weeks more, and we'd be back bright and early on surgery day.

Lizzie, Chris, and I tried to do fun things to take our minds off the surgery. The day before, we kept her home from school for a relaxing, fun day. Chris even took the day off, and we were determined to make the day wonderful. We took her to a movie she had been wanting to see, an animated movie. We took her to eat at her favorite Mexican food restaurant, because she loves the chips and salsa, and they make the "best" chicken tenders.

After our movie, and late lunch, we drove out to my favorite little chapel, about fifteen minutes outside of Austin. It sits on the side of a hill, overlooking little farms and houses, and has a beautiful view. It's a small chapel, open on three sides, used for weddings. It's not a church, but it is so peaceful, I feel drawn to the place. There is a giant bell inside a bell tower, that both Chris and Lizzie were always tempted to ring.

We arrived at the chapel, walked up the long sidewalk, and saw that it was empty. No wedding going on, thank goodness. I just wanted to sit. I wanted us to pray for Lizzie. I didn't really know how to pray, I never felt like I said the right things, but Chris did. There's a peace there, a calmness, and we needed this. Lizzie needed this. We sat, quietly, all praying for my girl. Praying for everything. Tomorrow was the day. We could feel it, we were finally there, surgery.

That night we tried and tried to sleep but it wasn't

happening. I read some prayers to Lizzie that a friend had written for us. I had told her of my fear of praying wrong, and she had taken the time to type out pages of prayer and scripture. It helped. The conflict was still very real to me inside, I believed God might be punishing me, and I was still terrified. I would try to tell myself to stop thinking the worst thoughts, it was too negative, but as surgery drew closer, the fear was very much alive and in charge.

We had to wake up at five o'clock and leave at five-forty-five in the morning. It was already after midnight, and it was impossible to sleep. I think we finally dozed off around one or two o'clock.

We left on time, and we took Chris's car, because he would be going back and forth, and we didn't know how long we would be at the hospital. The estimate was four days. There was no traffic, and we got there with no trouble, walked in, checked in, and Rachel showed up. We would wait for a while until they called us back to get her prepped. Ron and his new wife showed up. I tried not to let it affect me, for Lizzie's sake, but it was so difficult to be in the same room with him. The man who had taken a child from me, and had tried to take another. Very difficult. I had to stay strong.

They took us back to get her prepped, and we met the anesthesiologist, the nurses that would be taking care of her, and the man that would be monitoring her vitals and her spinal cord during the surgery.

They told us everything they were going to do, and said they would be screwing metal rods into her spine. I felt myself sinking.

It became too real. Hang on. Hang on.

Stay positive. No death. No death. I was doing my best to fight it. She'll be fine.

I couldn't help but think about Hannah, and her noticeable absence. I know she would want to be here, I kept thinking, surely she wanted to be here. Deep down I thought since she had seen all of us at the courthouse recently, it would have broken the ice a little bit, and she would be here. I was hoping. I was hoping she would be here, even if I was only able to see her, even if she still couldn't talk to me. I was prepared. I just wanted to see her. Why isn't she here? This is major surgery, there are major risks, am I the only reason she's not here? She should still be with her two sisters.

I had envisioned Hannah and Rachel strengthening their sisterly bond that day, I really thought this was going to be the day. This would be the thing that finally brought them back together as sisters. This was their baby, too, their little Lizzie. It was bothering me. It was getting to me. My girls have been ripped apart. I'm losing my children, that's what I was feeling, all of the loss, and it felt like death.

My baby was going into this horrible surgery in a few minutes. I was getting more nervous. They had given her Valium, and she was feeling fine. She was starting to say funny things, and everyone in the room was laughing. I wanted them to knock me out, too. Fast. Lizzie had been right, the first thing she told the doctor when he informed us about the need for surgery, "You'll have to knock my mom out, too." She was serious. She was right.

One last kiss on her forehead, one last "I love you," and it was time. They wheeled her out of the room and down the hall. I wasn't ready. I hoped I had told her I loved her enough. I hoped she knew I love her more than anything. I hoped she wasn't afraid. That was it. It would take over an hour to get her prepped, and the surgery would take at least six hours. Six hours of surgery, but maybe eight hours until she's completely done. Eight hours. Hang on.

My anxiety was getting bad, my body was tensed and I didn't feel right at all, and I was slowly losing control, already. I tried to act "normal." I tried not to show the fear. Chris, Rachel and I went to the cafeteria to get breakfast. I was going through the motions, my body was walking, but my mind was not there, it was with Lizzie. In my head all I could think of was what Lizzie was experiencing. What is she seeing, what are they doing to her now, what are they telling her, on and on in my thoughts, as I was holding a tray, choosing my breakfast. I was in two places, in those moments, this was the most bizarre feeling. Everything became magnified, and I was a little numb. It felt really strange. Looking back, I think the fear literally had me in it's grip, something you hear people say, but rarely experience for yourself.

They had given me a pager, the kind you get at restaurants while waiting for your table, that would light up if they couldn't reach you on your cell phone. I kept it right in front of me so I wouldn't miss anything. I had my phone sitting there, as well, and I kept staring at it. It had only been fifteen minutes, and already it felt like forever. This would be a very long day. Hang on. Be strong. Stay positive.

I was trying. My anxiousness was already getting the best of me. I was failing, already. I can't fail Lizzie today, I just can't do that.

Rachel, Chris and I ate breakfast sitting outside by a waterfall, and it was a little calming hearing the sound of falling water. As we were eating our meal, we saw Lizzie's anesthesiologist walk by, with his plate of food. We watched him through the windows as he walked to a little room where he joined other people dressed in scrubs.

"He's done with his part," Chris said. "She's had the anesthesia."

A chill went up and down my body.

My phone rang a little while later. It was the nurse from the operating room.

"Just wanted to let you know she's doing fine, the doctors are about to begin, and she's doing great," she said. She told me they loved her in the O.R., Lizzie had been wheeled into the room, and she was complimenting them on how awesome everything was. I knew she was expecting everything to be like what she sees on television, and in movies, and it made us all smile to hear she liked the operating room. That was our Lizzie.

She told me they would call me again after a while, but our girl was doing great. It was obvious by her tone, this was something she did every day, she had such a calm in her voice. I wanted her to keep talking to me, keep me in the room with Lizzie, by phone. It was an unrealistic and fleeting thought, but I needed to stay connected to Lizzie.

Time started blurring for me after that, the entire day is just little bits here and there. It already felt like it was taking an eternity, and had only been a couple of hours. My mom and sister showed up. They joined us in another area of the hospital, as we sat out in front of the coffee shop, near the gigantic entrance. The ceilings were really tall, and there were whimsical and beautiful pieces of art everywhere. The courtyard was gorgeous, and there was plenty to look at. I could listen to conversation, but it was tough to sit still. I wasn't really "there," I was off in another place in my mind, terrified, and sinking.

We passed the time talking, Chris and Rachel were at my side every second, and my mom and sister were there for support, and I was so grateful they were there. It was going as expected, it seemed, except for my failure. I hadn't really planned on things being this intense, and I had planned for intense. I saw myself being a little stronger, but I couldn't find any strength. I received another call, she was doing great. The surgery was going very well.

After a few hours, much of which I can barely remember, I got another call. The surgery was almost over, they were finishing sewing her incision. My body hurt. We would be called down soon to talk to the doctor.

We moved down to another area, near the O.R., to be available to talk to the doctor. Only Ron and I would be allowed to go in at this point. I wanted to bring Chris, but he couldn't go with me. We waited, and soon were taken back to a little room with a few chairs, a table, and a desk with a computer sitting on top. We waited.

I was sitting with Ron in a room, all alone. I tried to not look at him, and noticed someone had drawn a little cross on the whiteboard behind me. I wanted to scream at him, wanted to ask him how he can just sit there knowing what he had done. I couldn't look at him. I couldn't sit in this room with him for one more minute, it had been at least fifteen already.

I got up and walked out. I paced up and down the little hall, and waited for the doctor to show up. As soon as I saw him coming down the hall, I walked back into the little room. He entered the room, extended his hand to me and said everything went great, she was doing very well. Relief. Thank God, it's done, and she did well. No death. Total relief.

I pictured my sweet girl back there somewhere with God knows how many things, tubes, wires hooked into her little body, now with metal rods screwed into her spine. My body hurt. My head hurt.

He began to show us on the computer screen the work he had done in her back. All I saw through my teary eyes was an X-ray, and what looked like little white screws, and long metal rods. I was trying to listen. Suddenly Ron started talking about the heart attack he had experienced a few years before.

What? Your heart attack? My baby is lying back there about to wake up in complete agony, and now I have to hear about your heart attack?

No. Please stop.

It may have been a little dramatic, but I might have rolled my eyes, and made a loud, well, very loud "sigh." I couldn't help it. I just couldn't help myself. I couldn't take anymore. The doctor looked around quickly at me, and then continued talking, and thank goodness, he was the only one talking after that moment.

We finished with the doctor and I got out of that room as fast as I could. I went back out to Chris, and my group. Very soon after this we were all, including Ron, his wife, and her mother, all escorted back to yet another area. This would be the final waiting room, close to the Intensive Care Unit that Lizzie would be taken to shortly.

The waiting. Be strong. Hang on. Stay positive.

A woman came to get us after a while, by this time it had been over eight hours since we had seen Lizzie. I knew it would be difficult to see her, I was trying to brace myself for the worst.

As we walked in the room, there she was. My Lizzie. It was good to see her, but oh my gosh, it was awful. I don't think I've ever felt anything for another human being, as I did at this moment. Her little face was all swollen, she was hooked up to every kind of tube, wire, monitor, more than I had even imagined. I bent down and kissed her forehead gently. Everyone filed into the room. Everyone just looked at her. I don't remember how long it took for her to really wake up, but when she did, I got down close to her face, and she looked up at me with pure terror in her eyes.

"Mom, it hurts so bad," she cried, with panic.

"I didn't know it was going to hurt this bad," she cried, with more terror on her face.

So much fear. So much pain. I couldn't do anything. Nothing. Help. Help me. Help her. Somebody do something!

I was near the edge. I could feel it.

I knew I had to be strong, for Lizzie. Be positive, for Lizzie. Keep it together for her, but it's too much.

It was completely overwhelming, but I was trying. She was in so much pain. My little girl who never complains, always has a positive attitude, is being tortured. Why? Why does she have to suffer?

She was alive, I was grateful, but why are they letting her feel so much pain?

Chris was attentive, there for me, my rock. As long as he was there, I had something to hold on to.

Chapter 16

The first night, we were told, would be the worst. We were trying to prepare for whatever this meant, and I couldn't even imagine everything getting worse. Rachel didn't want to leave, but had to go home, she was in the process of moving. Ron and his wife, her mother, my mom and sister, all finally left. Chris would go home to take care of things. That left only me, the weakest one of the group, alone with Lizzie.

There she was, my Lizzie, in agony. She had moments that were better, when we would have a little conversation. At one point she wanted me to take a video of her explaining how she was doing. She wanted to remember everything she went through. We would be in ICU for at least twenty-four hours. The nurses were wonderful, our first was a really sweet young man. He was caring, efficient, and sweet to Lizzie. We were at their mercy. I felt so helpless to make her more comfortable.

I pulled the reclining chair as close to her as I possibly could without getting in the way of the nurse, and to let her know I was right there for her. Pain, so much pain. She was on Morphine, and a handful of other pain medications, and was still in so much pain.

As the night went on, her pain became worse. I would doze off for a few minutes, and she would call out to me. I couldn't do anything but tell her I was sorry, that was it. I'm sorry. Helpless.

Every hour the nurse and an aid would come in to

rotate her from side to side, they didn't want her on her back for too long. Just holding her hand hurt her, so you can imagine what rolling her entire body was doing to her. Pure agony, every hour or so. This went on throughout the night. When she fell asleep, I dozed off, for about an hour. I awoke in the middle of a light sleep, and saw someone coming towards me with some type of blanket, like they were going to cover me up. I quickly realized it was a lead apron, to protect me. They were going to X-ray Lizzie's chest, because something wasn't right. Her oxygen level was way too low, something was wrong with her lungs. It was caused by the anesthesia, and they would start her on breathing treatments. It was hard for her, she struggled with the machine, it hurt her. More pain.

We made it through the first night, Lizzie was getting really good at pushing the Morphine button. She could give herself a dose every fifteen minutes, and there would be a little noise if it was getting into her I.V., to let her know she got the dose.

She pushed it constantly, and much too often. My girl was suffering. I could do nothing. I told her I wish it were me, suffering, and not her. "Oh, mom, you couldn't handle this," in her typical way. She always felt she could handle anything that came her way, and it was just one of her many admirable characteristics. Her soul was old. I've always said there's a little old lady living inside of her.

People began showing up again that morning, Chris, Rachel, Ron and his wife, my mom and sister. Later in the day a woman brought a sweet therapy dog to visit, named Ariel, and for the first time Lizzie's face lit up with a smile. It was good therapy for everyone, to see her smile. Thank God, a smile. Ariel was a beautiful, and sweet, sweet Australian Shepherd. She jumped up on a chair, and gently put her two front paws on the bed next to

Lizzie. She knew to be gentle, it was the sweetest thing I've ever seen. She had purpose, simply to love Lizzie.

Lizzie reached up to pet her, and smiled. Her fur was so soft, and it was heart warming to watch the effect it had on our girl. She loved Ariel, and for a few moments, she was able to focus on something other than her pain.

The physical therapy team came in late that day, to get Lizzie up on her feet. I was in a bit of shock, that they were going to make her stand up. They asked everyone to leave the room, except for me, and Lizzie asked Rachel to stay. They said there was a possibility she would get very sick when she stood up. She did. It was awful. But she stood, for at least a minute.

When everyone came back into the room, Chris pulled me aside. He was feeling sick, and didn't think he should be there around Lizzie. With everything going on, I was a bit angry and upset he was leaving me, but knew he was right. I told him to go home. The doctor told us we would most likely be here for four days, and surgery day was considered day zero, so we were only at day one. I figured we had three more days of this, and would be released, with Chris helping us once we got home. It would be fine.

Her oxygen level was still too low, but we made it finally, to our own room. There was still an issue with her lungs, and they were still doing the breathing treatments, all day long. We were making progress, and we would now have a little more privacy. I couldn't wait for the quiet to kick in. I had only had a little bit of sleep, and my head was beginning to feel very foggy. The anxiety was steadily growing, everything began to annoy me, and Chris wasn't there to calm me.

Lizzie began to receive flowers and gifts. We tried to focus on the positives, and progress so that we could go home. There was a checklist of things that had to happen over the next couple of days, and if everything went well we could go home. Home.

Day three, Chris didn't come back, but everyone else was still there. I knew he wasn't feeling well, and didn't want to risk giving Lizzie whatever he had. I was exhausted, I hadn't had more than an hour of sleep at a time, and maybe three in total every night. I was trying to do everything right.

I was getting more and more frustrated with Lizzie's pain, over the next twenty-four hours she was feeling all of the tubes, and the needles in her body. She said she could feel the metal rods they had placed in her back.

My anxiety was in full gear now, I was beginning to feel irritated at everything, annoyed my child was in this horrible situation. They had taken her morphine away, her button, which she now called her "best friend." As they were taking it, she said it was the end of an era, and she would mourn the loss. She still had her sense of humor, thank goodness. That night, still no sleep, only a little here and there.

By day four, I was getting delirious. I was venting to Chris over the phone, and he was frustrated he couldn't be there, and was back at work. He would try to tell me what to do, I know he tried to make it better, but I became defensive and couldn't take the direction from him. He was supposed to be my rock, get me through. I was starting to feel sick as well, and thought maybe it was from lack of sleep. My throat then began to hurt, and I knew I was getting sick, hoping it wasn't anything that Lizzie could catch.

Ron and his wife had been coming and going every day, and when they were there, they mostly sat and looked at their phones. There really wasn't much we could do. I would try to get on Facebook and reply to messages people were sending, and try to keep busy. I was drowning. I didn't feel well at all. I was frustrated my cell phone wasn't getting good service, and Chris had been trying to call. He thought I wasn't answering his calls, and by the time I called him, he was angry. Our anxiety was high.

When I heard the anger in his voice, my rock, angry, my rock that was supposed to get me through, no matter what, I became angry. He had told me he was going to help us get through this nightmare. He said he had my back, and not to worry. Now he's angry at me? I vented everything straight to him. I suddenly felt myself explode, and I told him to get out of my life, and I hung up. I didn't mean it. I didn't really mean to say what I said. I was frustrated, and completely out of my mind. I wasn't myself at all, and hadn't been in such a long time, that this stressful situation brought out the worst kind of monster.

I was a mess. I tried hard to put a good face on, but I was a mess inside. I just wanted to be able to take Lizzie home now. They had told us about four days from surgery day, which meant tomorrow. Poor girl, one hand filled up and swelled with liquid from the I.V., and they had to start a new one. I had told her they would do all of this while she was knocked out before surgery, and now, they were putting a new one in her forearm. She was tortured, already feeling like she had been stabbed all over.

I tried to call Chris the next day, and no answer. Day four at the hospital, I needed him. I knew I had been horrible to him, I knew he was ignoring me. Surely he knew I hadn't meant what I said. I sent text messages to him. I texted him more. No answers.

Day five came and went. Lizzie still couldn't keep her oxygen up, and we had a couple of other issues, but they began to take some of her older I.V.'s out, and some other tubes.

Everyone had left the day before, and were not coming back, because we thought we would be going home. Rachel began spending the night in the room with us, and would "take over" caring for Lizzie, and I was able to sleep three hours in a row. She would bring dinner for me. I was eating a salad with walnuts, and felt pain shooting throughout my head, I had broken a tooth. Wonderful. I was trying so hard to be strong and well for Lizzie, but the world was doing a fantastic job of beating me up. I needed sleep, real rest, desperately. Lizzie had made me promise not to leave her side, before we even arrived at the hospital for surgery, "Do not leave me, mom." Every time I wanted to run and escape, her words hit me. I was doing my best.

Rachel and I traded each night, one of us would get the chair, an upright chair with no recline, and the other would get the little "sofa," two cushions that would pull out to make a "bed." Neither were comfortable. One night I decided to sleep in the wheelchair we had in the room, because it reclined. I slept about three hours that night.

Day six, Lizzie was beginning to decline a little bit. They still wouldn't let us go home, and I was getting nervous, we were already two days over what we had been told. Rachel would come and go, and bring dinner and movies. We were trying to pass the time, and keep Lizzie entertained. I still couldn't get Chris to answer his phone. I was getting really worried. In the back of my mind, I knew he'd be at my house waiting for us, ready to dote on Lizzie, and I would rest. I wasn't thinking straight, my thoughts were completely irrational.

Day seven. We needed to go home. Rachel and I decided to take Lizzie outside to a courtyard, in the wheelchair. Fresh air. We thought maybe some fresh air would help our girl, and pick her spirits up so we could go home. We pushed her slowly down the hall and outside, every little bump would make her hurt even worse. The pain. She had so much pain.

It worked. The doctor came to tell us later, he would release her. Good news. We were running out of energy, running out of hope, and finally, we could get out of there. Rachel and I began to pack up the room, and get organized. We still had to wait for the doctor's assistant to demonstrate how to change Lizzie's bandages, but we were ready to go. They took out the last I.V., the new one they had just put in her arm, because her vein had failed. At last, no more needles. Her little arms were covered in cotton and band-aids.

Finally, our last step, the bandages. The assistant came in with supplies, and we rolled Lizzie on to her side. This always hurt her, but it had to be done, we had to get the bandage off. It looked like a huge sheet of yellow glue, over a foot wide and eighteen inches long, up and down her entire back. She began to rip the "glue" at the very top on Lizzie's shoulder, and Lizzie screamed. She grabbed more, and began to rip it off, pulling the skin all around on Lizzie's back.

By the time she had been working for ten minutes or so, she had hardly taken any of it off. Lizzie was screaming in pain. What? Now, when we finally get to go home, we torture her more? I have never heard my child make the sounds she was making, in all of her twelve years. Never. It was excruciating to hear. Rachel was holding her hand, Lizzie was squeezing her as hard as she could. Crying. We were crying. I was trying to watch, but I was crying and couldn't see.

The nurse finally stepped in and told the assistant she would try. She used some little adhesive remover pads and slowly was able to get the rest of the glue off of Lizzie's back, which was now bright red. I could see the incision, covered with little strips of tape, it looked over a foot long. My body hurt just looking at it. My sweet baby girl.

She was shivering, quiet, still holding Rachel's hand. She was crying softly now. I had never seen my child suffer like this. It was more than overwhelming. We had to sit, helpless, and let them do this to her, and could do nothing but watch the torture.

After our traumatic send off at the hospital, Rachel, still taking charge, pulled her car up to the front. We loaded all of our things, flowers, gifts, and ever so gently and slowly placed Lizzie, still in her little hospital gown, into the back seat. We surrounded her with pillows, and strapped her in. Everything was hurting her.

Rachel mapped out the best way home, and drove as carefully as possible, trying not to hit any bumps or holes in the road. Every little bump sent pain through Lizzie. We rolled the windows down to try to keep her from getting car sick. We had a little bucket in her lap, just in case. It was an intense car ride, lasting for about forty-five minutes, but seemed like hours.

Just get home. Chris will help. Still not answering his phone, or text messages, I knew he would be there. He'll help, I knew he would help. He would never let Lizzie down. He did not have children of his own, and repeatedly said Lizzie was the only child he would ever consider his own. He loved her. He would be there, waiting. We had decided he would be in charge of having balloons and flowers waiting for Lizzie at home, to accompany the large Teddy Bear we had bought for her.

All I could think of now was Lizzie's face when she walked into our home, greeted with more balloons, more flowers, and the Teddy Bear. Something happy to look forward to. I fantasized about getting Lizzie home, comfortable, and finally being able to collapse into Chris's arms . . . and rest. I needed rest.

We got home, to our second floor apartment outside the city, in the country air. It was a peaceful place, temporary until we could buy a house. I was nervous about the stairs, but the physical therapist had made Lizzie walk up and down four stairs outside the hospital wing we were on, to make sure she knew she could do it.

When we were lifting her up from the back seat of the car, we noticed the pillows, and her gown were literally glued to her back. The left over glue from the bandage, mixed with the heat from the air, and sitting in the car, had literally glued her to everything. We had to sit and slowly peel everything away from her already sore skin, and it was hurting her. My poor child. Suffering, even more. It was more than any of us could comprehend. Obstacles at every turn. Will it ever end? We needed something to be easy, a bright spot in this nightmare.

We made our way up the stairs, very slowly, but she did it. When we walked into the apartment, I quickly looked around for the balloons . . . where are the balloons? Where are the flowers? I thought maybe he would bring them after he got off work, since they weren't there. Still not thinking clearly, I was trying to get Lizzie settled. We made it to the bed finally, and tried to get her as comfortable as possible. She was so glad to be home.

We gave her pain medicine and let her rest.

I began to notice that none of Chris's things were

lying around. My mind still wasn't working right, I hadn't slept in a week, and I was still feeling sick from whatever allergies I was having. I couldn't think straight. I looked closer, and saw that everything he had brought over, was gone. He was gone.

He was gone, and I had told him to leave.

What have I done? It hurts. The pain is too much.

How will I survive? I can't do this without him. How could he do this to me? How could he do this to Lizzie? No!

My fear. My anger. My mouth.

He was gone. Loss.

Please, no.

Chapter 17

Lizzie was finally resting comfortably at home, and she was taking strong narcotics to help with her pain, which was still agonizing. You couldn't even lightly touch the bed without her feeling it. I had to do everything for her, but she could walk, slowly, and with someone holding both of her arms. Rachel and I would walk backwards, gently holding on to her and guiding her. We made her walk as much as possible, just as we were told. After a few minutes, she would be exhausted, and in pain. It was like having a newborn baby all over again. Up every four hours for pain medication, helping her do everything, catering to her every need.

It kept me distracted for most of the day, but when she would fall asleep, I would fall apart. I was calling Chris every chance I got, with no answer. I left a voice mail, which was probably hard to understand because I was sobbing throughout the entire message. My text messages went from anger to sweetness, asking him to come back, and then anger again when he wouldn't answer. I needed him. Lizzie needed him. How could he do this?

Because I told him to.

A couple of days went by, and my tears would not stop. I had no control over my tears, they would just flow down my face, no matter what I was doing. I would be talking to Lizzie, tears pouring out of my eyes, and she would pretend not to notice after a while. I had finally slept for about four hours, twice in one night, and was beginning to feel a little more normal.

Every day the challenge was keeping Lizzie comfortable. I had to stay as strong as possible, but I was completely falling apart, in every way.

Chris was gone. I had told him to go. I kept having to remind myself I had told him to go. I didn't even feel like that same person I had been that day. We were home now, back in our own little world, and I had been a total wreck, so lost at the hospital, trying to survive.

My anxiety was higher than it had ever been, my sadness deeper, my fear greater, and I had never felt so alone in my entire life. I had nothing to grab hold of, nothing to land on. I had always been a survivor, always had something pushing me, but somehow I had finally lost my footing in the world. My heart was broken. I was reaching for anything, it was pure anguish. Anguish, and I had asked for it. Somehow I had to be strong for Lizzie, but I didn't have any strength.

Rachel had spent the first couple of nights at home with us, she was our hero, with super powers, energy, she had really stepped up and been there for us. She finally had to go back to her life, her job, her new house she had just moved into to the day of surgery. She said she would be back in a few days. That first night she had gone home, we were alone. Lizzie fell asleep again really late, she would sleep about four hours until the pain would wake her. We did our best to stay ahead of the pain.

It was warm outside, and I decided to sit out on the patio. All I could hear was the humming of the air conditioning units below me. The sky was beautifully lit up with stars, it was gorgeous. I thought of Chris, and how I had needed him at the hospital. All the nights leading up to the surgery when he told me he would be there for me,

"I got this," he would say, comforting me. I thought of our last conversation, and how all the days at the hospital were a blur now. I was trying desperately to remember every single detail of when I had last talked to Chris. I hadn't slept very much in over a week, and my brain was not functioning well at all. Nothing made sense. I began to get emotional, angry, and confused.

I began to feel an enormous amount of guilt, and shame. I thought about Hannah, and how I had acted when I felt I was losing her. I could never grasp what was happening at the time, and I began to act irrational. I became more angry, more emotional. I had felt my heart was being ripped out, trampled, destroyed. I missed her. I wanted her back. I wanted her to be close to her sisters again. It wasn't fair. I was angry.

I missed my dad. I wanted a hug from my dad. Our family was no longer a family. I needed Chris. I've lost Chris. My behavior was inexcusable, I knew it was my fault he left. The guilt. My poor Lizzie. She's lying in there with such a long road ahead of her. Why? Why has everything happened this way? I wanted to scream. Everything felt like death to me now, every loss was a total loss, and I did not handle any loss with grace or dignity. The pain was real and overwhelming.

I am being punished. God is punishing me. I'm a terrible person. I've run everyone off. I've hurt people. I'm angry, bitter, defensive. I'm a mess. I'm alone. I'm all alone because I was so horrible. Maybe Ron was right, I thought, nobody could ever love me, I was unlovable. My thoughts and emotions were all over the place. I was confused, and couldn't decide what was real and what wasn't. I could not focus on one thought, it felt like my mind was literally under attack.

The pain was excruciating. I had messed up

everything in my life. I thought that everything was my fault. The guilt, the shame, the hurt all at once. I had always managed to find my way out of the messes before, I always found a detour around obstacles. I had finally hit a "dead end." There was nothing in front of me, no side street, no way out. This was a new experience, nothing I had felt before, just the end of everything. The end.

It finally built up and boiled over the top, everything exploded. My head felt like it was literally going to break. I felt all of this heaviness, this pressure running from my head down my back. My spirit was crushed. I was done. I could not breathe. I didn't have anywhere else to go, but down.

There I found myself, down on my knees, all broken into a thousand pieces. Then, slumped down on the ground leaning on the metal railing of the patio, crying out to God telling Him how awful I was, and how sorry I was. "God, I'm sorry. I'm sorry. I'm so sorry." It's all I could say. I was defeated. Life had crushed me. I had failed everyone. I had reached my limit.

After a while, I had nothing left to say, and couldn't feel anything, and my body was just shuttering. A certain peace fell over me. A peace I had not ever remembered feeling before. Just total peace. No anxiety, no feeling, no pain. As my life of memories paraded across my mind, certain things would get to me, another gentle cry and some guilt. My emotions would fight against each other deep inside, but I had no energy to bother with any of it. I was just staring up at stars, it was like watching a movie in my head, not thinking with any purpose.

What was happening? Something was happening, but I couldn't understand what it was. I felt different. It felt like I was being "filled up" with peace. That little feeling I had so many times before that something awful was happening, or about to happen, or I was "knowing" something, this was this same feeling, only stronger. I was completely exhausted, not an ounce of energy for anything else, but somehow got up and made my way inside, and laid down on the sofa. I flipped through the guide on television, and that night I stumbled upon a Joyce Meyer show, totally by accident, and decided to record future shows. I thought it might be good for me, I certainly couldn't get out to go to church anytime soon, Lizzie and I would be home for weeks. I watched for a little while, and had written down a few verses, to look up later. I needed sleep.

The next day, whenever Lizzie would fall asleep I would look up the verses. Some of them I needed for comfort, but some of them made me realize how much I had failed. More guilt piled on top of existing guilt.

I found an empty little notebook, a miniature composition book, about three inches by five inches. I began to write everything I read that touched me, into this little book. On the first page I wrote something Chris had told me, "God's plan . . . is the best plan," which he had found in a restroom at a gas station when we were out one day, and taken a picture of it. Whoever had written it on the wall, had very nice handwriting, and the background color looked like an old yellowed piece of paper. It was actually very nicely done.

I wrote Bible verses that I had heard on television. I wrote things I saw friends post on Facebook, and then I started searching on the internet how to pray. I always felt I didn't pray right. I was always afraid someone would ask me to say a prayer at dinner, when I was visiting family, or friends. I can remember feeling awkward about this a few times in my life. I had heard of that happening to other people, and knew the fear.

I searched how to pray for forgiveness, love, strength, comfort, everything I could think of. I found hundreds and hundreds of people who could pray correctly. They would write the most beautifully written prayers, and I would copy some of them down in my little book, adjusting them slightly to fit my own troubles.

I would carry that little notebook around with me all day long, reading it, praying out loud. It was my security, or a dose of medicine for my "illness." If I began to feel afraid, I had a couple verses and prayers for courage, comfort, and I would read every page I had written over and over. I would search for more things to write in my little book, I couldn't stop looking for things I needed. I could not get enough. I had never acted this way, had never done this before, but it felt like what I was supposed to do.

I began to write little notes on our bathroom mirror with dry erase markers, and tape little notes around the house. I had to have it in front of my eyes all day long or I would fall apart. I was still having really high "highs," and really low "lows." My emotions were up and down, all over the place. But I felt more peace, for more of the day. It didn't happen instantly, but I was beginning to feel a little better each day. I still couldn't figure out what was happening to me, but it felt completely wonderful, whatever it was.

I was still sending text messages to Chris, and I was starting to believe he really was gone forever. If I started to feel any anxiety about it, I would grab my little book, and pray all of the prayers out loud. I would pray for him. I had never prayed like this in my life.

On one occasion, I became really angry, was having a very low "low," and I sat and blasted him in a text message. I said horrible things. I was frustrated and angry, and afraid. I said as many hurtful things as I could say. I couldn't stop myself. He had abandoned me, when I needed him most. He had abandoned Lizzie, which was even more shocking and painful. I called him all sorts of terrible things. I wanted to hurt him.

The next day, I was watching one of the recorded Joyce Meyer shows, and she named a verse, Ephesians 4:15. I wrote it down in a larger spiral notebook I had started, for my "studying", but instead of 4:15, I mistakenly wrote 4:29. Quickly after I wrote it, I looked up at the screen, and realized my mistake. As I erased the 29, and was writing 15, something told me I needed to see what 29 said, just in case. I hit pause, and went to read 29, and there it was. "Do not let any unwholesome talk come out of your mouths, but only what is helpful for building others up according to their needs, that it may benefit those who listen."

I immediately, instantaneously, thought of the mean, horrible text I had sent to Chris. I felt awful. I knew at this moment, God, or the angel He had sent to baby-sit my pitiful, emotional, erratic self, was guiding me. I knew it. I said a prayer of thanks and gratitude, and asked for forgiveness. I felt something I had always felt, this guidance, but had assumed before, this was my intuition, or my psychic ability, or all the weirdness I thought I was. I realized, there might be a slight possibility I wasn't psychic at all. Was it God all those times before?

Little things kept happening, little "coincidences," at least once, sometimes twice a day. I would be experiencing something, and suddenly, there was a message about that very thing, on some form of social media, or television. I would be talking to a friend, and they would say something I had just experienced, or had just thought about. I would meet someone at the grocery store that told me something a friend had told me the night before, or I had just read somewhere. It was happening constantly, and I was feeling it, appreciating it with all of my heart. It was so comforting. It gave me peace I had never known, and it kept getting better.

Lizzie was improving daily. I was praying for her. Praying for Rachel, and Hannah, my family, and Chris. I stopped watching anything negative on television, only positive, uplifting shows, that would give me energy. I was reading everything I could, studying everything I could find. I couldn't stop. It was a craving I had never had before, an insatiable craving, and it was helping me, helping me stay calm.

1 Peter 2:2 "Like newborn babies you should crave (thirst for, earnestly desire) the pure (unadulterated) spiritual milk, that by it you may be nurtured and grow into completed salvation."

It says it right there in the Bible, exactly what was happening to me. When I read that verse, I couldn't believe it. It's the way I felt, the way I was acting, I could not get enough of this knowledge. The way it was changing my thoughts and feelings was incredible. It was not only changing my thoughts and feelings, but changing my life! I had never experienced anything so incredible before, this exceeded even the most intense of the bizarre experiences I had in the past. This moment was probably one of the most important of my new journey, it was confirmation that everything was real. It was very real. It wasn't just in my head, it wasn't anything I was inventing or imagining, this was real.

God was helping me, I could feel it. It was a supernatural thing that was happening, something I had never imagined could happen. I never believed you could actually "feel" God. I saw a picture a friend had posted on

Facebook, "God uses pain and brokenness to lead our hearts to repentance and love," by Wendy Blight. This was so real. I was in pain, I was broken into pieces, and He is there, He is really helping me.

My emotions would still take over, but I now had knowledge to fight any pain or anxiety that would begin to affect me. The little notes all around the house helped, and I continued to add new messages every day. Lizzie finally asked, with a smile, "should I expect more of these messages?" I knew Rachel noticed, and was politely keeping comments to herself. I needed these reminders, all day, but it was working. I still added verses, and prayers to my little book, which was almost full. I would sit and read through the entire book, at least a couple of times a day now. I felt strength, peace, courage to go on with life. I hadn't felt this strong in years.

A couple of short weeks after the night I was broken down, I felt so much better, and people noticed. Lizzie's Home Bound teacher, Diana, actually told me I seemed like a completely different person, from only a couple of weeks before. It was obvious. I was grateful.

Psalm 34:18 "The Lord is close to the brokenhearted and saves those who are crushed in spirit."

That was me, and He did save me. Little old average me, who had ignored Him for so long, and who had been so ungrateful for my life. How in the world could God possibly love me this much? Why me?

I was still hurting over Chris, I missed him, and I had little reminders of him everywhere. I had been collecting little rocks on our hikes, for months, little rocks shaped like hearts. One day he had called me from work and said he had found a great rock for me. He brought it home, and it was an enormous rock, shaped like a heart. It was the sweetest thing.

As I sat now, day after day, looking at that heart-shaped rock, I would become emotional. I couldn't look at it anymore, but couldn't bear to let it go just yet. I decided to put the cross symbol on it, to change it. I got a little tool out and literally scraped and scraped until I had carved a large cross on the front of the rock.

Two days later, I saw a picture on a Bible page on Facebook, and it said "I always thought love was shaped like a heart but it's actually like a cross," with little symbols for a heart and a cross. I couldn't believe it, the timing was incredible. About two days later, Diana came over to help Lizzie, and told me a previous student of hers had finally received the new heart he had been waiting for. He was a spiritual boy, about Lizzie's age, and had undergone heart-transplant surgery. She loved what I had done to the rock, and asked if she could send the boy a picture of my rock, and the picture I found on Facebook. I was thrilled.

Just another confirmation to me that everything was happening as it should. Most importantly, God was with me. I really couldn't believe He was with me, me, of all people, after I had been such a terrible person, and was never a real, true Christian. God wasn't only with me, He was working in my life, loving me up and I could see it, and actually feel it.

Chapter 18

I woke up one morning, feeling almost completely rested, because Lizzie was sleeping more now. She was doing very well. We had our first check-up since surgery, and everything looked good. We were having a couple of new little issues with pain and sensitivity, but overall, she was doing very well. Relief. We were conquering Scoliosis. Her spine would never be completely straight, but the difference in her posture was obvious. Since her surgery, she had gained over an inch in height, which she loved to hear. Life was starting to seem a little good again. Her teacher, Diana, was coming twice a week, and Lizzie was able to get more and more work done. We were going to make it.

I had been drinking my morning coffee, and looking through some pictures on the Bible page on Facebook again, and something reached out to me. It said "Sometimes the best ways to share our faith is to simply share our lives and our stories." It spoke to me. I had for years, decades now, had a longing, a strong desire to write a book. I had started writing books probably four or five times since my twenties. Me, the girl who had failed English, and failed out of high school. Me.

In all of my previous attempts, I had written at least one hundred pages, sometimes almost two hundred. I could never come up with a way to end it, and couldn't decide on a title, or sometimes even a beginning. I had started, and stopped so many times. I had re-written and thrown away pages and pages of writing because I would hate it as soon as I wrote it.

Something was very different this time, I felt a new confidence. This would be my story, it was still about all the crazy things that had happened to me over the years, but there would be a new twist. My story now had a point! It was clear in my head, for the first time. Maybe this is what God wants me to do, maybe this is what He has wanted all along, I thought, and my friend Meredith had the same exact thought. Maybe this is where my new life is heading, and this is what I was supposed to write, all this time. I decided to try, since Lizzie and I were going to be confined at home for a few weeks, this might be perfect timing. I would write about what has happened, and what God has done for me.

I sat down with my laptop and wrote out a title. Then a subtitle, and suddenly I had written eight pages. I was already thinking ahead, and it was clear. This wouldn't be a novel, like I had tried to write before, it would simply be my story. I truly believe it is what God wanted me to write. I know some people might not believe it, but after so many attempts before, and the clarity I was experiencing now, there really isn't any other explanation. It's nothing I would have ever written before now, if I hadn't had "the night," the meltdown, this would have never been written. Bad or good, it wasn't anything I would have thought of writing. I was shocked at how fast it was pouring out of me, and I was grateful. Constantly grateful.

Soon I had written thirty or forty pages, very quickly. I was telling Meredith about it, and would read a little to her. She liked it. She gave me more confidence. I would read a bit to Lizzie, and she would giggle or tear up, in the right places, and I felt even better. I had never written like this in my life. It felt right. It was my heart and soul, my life, the good and the bad, and even all the humiliating parts. When I wrote all those times before, I tried to write more anonymously, something I felt more comfortable doing. Now, it was as if I couldn't humiliate myself enough, but it was right. I knew this was what I was supposed to do.

I was beginning to realize my anxiety, my fear, my bitterness was all fading away a little, with each page I wrote. I had held grudges, not even realizing I was holding grudges. I was carrying around baggage from thirty years ago, twenty years ago, and it was just all piled up on top of me, weighing me down. I didn't even realize it, until I began shedding these weights off, one by one. It's shocking when you realize exactly how trapped you've been, only when you've been set free.

As I was writing, I was forgiving everyone and everything I was writing about. Forgiveness, I now understood not only what it was, but how it actually frees your soul. Forgiveness. I had heard the word a million times, but never in my life, not once, did I remember actually feeling what it felt like to really forgive someone. I thought I had forgiven people before, but never like this new, thoughtful forgiveness. The release of anger and hurt that had built up for decades, now leaving my soul. It was indescribable.

I had always heard of people forgiving their enemies, and could never really understand how they actually did it, or to be completely honest, why they would want to forgive an enemy. People would even tell me they had done it, especially Chris, he was the fastest forgiver I had ever met. He could forgive anyone, for anything. I really never experienced this before. I was forgiving so many things, but knew there were a couple of people that would present a struggle for me. I wasn't sure I could actually forgive those people who had caused the most pain. I put those aside, and worked on the rest for the moment. This was all happening so quickly, and I knew I wanted to do things right, in the eyes of God.

How awesome of God to use my desire to write, to actually start to heal me, and show me what forgiveness truly felt like. The more I wrote, the more I healed and learned, and some days I still couldn't believe it. What a wonderful gift I had been given. Gratitude. Lots and lots of gratitude.

I was feeling so much joy, after being in such a dark, negative place, with absolutely no hope. I was also studying more and more. For the first time, I was reading Bible verses that actually applied directly to a feeling, thought, or an emotion I was having. I had tried before to read the Bible, always starting at the beginning and trying to read it through like a novel. It never worked, I would get frustrated, distracted, and quit. This time I was getting it, I was understanding what I was reading, and I would feel my connection with God becoming stronger, and stronger. This was all happening so fast, I couldn't believe how fast. I had always used music in this way, to satisfy different moods, or emotions I was having, but it was nothing like this, nothing as powerful as what was happening to me now.

I would sit outside and sip hot tea, and stare at the sky when Lizzie was sleeping, in amazement at how everything in my past, my present, all of the workings of my life were colliding into this beautiful explosion of goodness. All of this providing a peace I had never felt, and a new purpose, one I had only failed at so many times before, writing my story. This time I had clarity, focus, guidance, and I could feel it, it was finally happening.

As I sat one night, outside, I was praying to God, and thinking of my dad, my little lady friend, and Chris's mom, all deceased, and had the most peaceful feeling come over me. I prayed that I hoped they were all with me, and Chris. I walked inside for a moment, and came back out just in time to see a falling star. It was very low in the sky, and seemed to be right in front of me, meant for me to see. It felt wonderful. I was continually receiving little signs of encouragement, and reassurances. Again, I knew God was working.

For the first time in my life, I really believed that God was with me, and actually making things happen in my life. It took me fifty years, a lot of heartache, loss, guilt, bad decisions, loads and loads of fear and anxiety, and no religion, but I found my way to God. No more doubt, absolutely no more.

Revelation 21:4 "He will wipe away every tear from their eyes, and death shall be no more, neither shall there be mourning, nor crying, nor pain anymore, for the former things have passed away."

I wasn't at the end of my life, but this is how I was feeling, that all of the former things had passed away. For the first time I wasn't carrying my entire life's worth of baggage around with me all day.

He had given me peace, taken away almost all of my anxiety, every bit of my depression, and all of the negative influences that were keeping me stuck. I was stuck in a place, a very negative place, that had been progressively getting more negative as the years passed. I didn't feel paralyzed with depression anymore, or haunted by the past, or tormented by anxiety. I realized that I hadn't been doing any of the things I needed to do to get out, and this little bit of peace I was now feeling gave me a new understanding of what I needed to do.

I needed to keep writing, keep studying, keep praying, but mostly keep being grateful for all of these wonderful things God was doing for me. He was mending my heart, my life. Thanking him constantly, praying all day for other people, especially my children, something I had never done before, ever. Keep it going, don't lose focus, this was the goal.

I still prayed for God to bring Chris back to me, to change his heart, to just bring him back. I needed him, and I will do better this time. I will love like I'm supposed to love. I won't be negative. I prayed and prayed. I was still so sad I had pushed him away, and begged God to bring him back to me. I learned through reading prayers of other people, and talking with Meredith and Diana, that I should pray for something only "if it's in my best interest," and only if it's "God's plan." This became the daily prayer.

Chapter 19

I'm sure you've heard it a thousand times in your life, at least, to "Turn everything over to God," and, "Put everything in God's hands." I know I've heard it plenty of times myself. Something always bothered me about this, I thought it was actually burdening God. I thought God had plenty to do, there were bigger things going on that needed His attention, and that I would be bothering Him with my drama.

That's honestly how I felt. I'm ashamed now to say, I actually argued with someone years ago, and couldn't believe she actually thought God knew about all the little things in her life. I had friends who were praying for a new, or better car, or for something material, and I thought that was ridiculous. In my own way of thinking, I believed I should only ask God to save someone from a life-threatening accident or illness, or if someone needed real help. This is really the only reason I would ever "pray," in my own little way, my own little wrong way.

To turn your whole life, all the drama, the insignificant silly things, the desires for material things, well, I just thought that was all pretty selfish, and not to mention, difficult. How in the world do you turn your life over, when you've been trying everything you can think of, just to hang on to life? That would take an awful lot of courage. When Meredith and another friend told me that we're supposed to, that it was what God wants you to do, I somehow began to trust them, and see the other perspective. When I heard Joyce Meyer say the same thing, I thought it had to be the right thing to do. When you turn everything over to Him, you will more likely be on your predestined path. Simple enough. I tried it, I prayed to God, to take everything in my life and change it into something He wanted it to be. I was finally beginning to understand the whole concept, and once again, realizing how backwards my own beliefs had been.

I wasn't blaming myself, but I was a little more than upset that I never had all of this wonderful knowledge before, when I needed it so badly. I could have avoided so many of the negative things that had been crushing me. I always believed in God, but I was merely following what I thought were "signs" from God. Looking back, I realized I didn't even do that very well. I was wrong about almost everything.

So there I was, now turning everything over to God, to the best of my ability. I could hear the influences of the past in my head, "People who are weak use God and religion as a crutch." I had heard that since I was a child. It was a bit of a struggle, but I knew this new truth now, and couldn't believe how wrong those influences of my past really were. Sadly, I had let them shape my beliefs. Here I was, giving everything to God. It felt great! I prayed it over and over, to keep myself on track. All of the things that had defeated me, made me feel like life had gotten the best of me, those were the things I focused on. The "big" hurts, the biggest obstacles, these things that kept me down, I was now trying to let it all go and turn it over to Him.

Very soon after this, maybe even the next day, I ran to the store while Lizzie was resting. I was in a great mood, it was a beautiful sunny day, Lizzie was doing very well. Things felt right. As I was out and about, I kept feeling this joy inside of me, and I was smiling without even trying. I have always been a friendly person, I could always talk to anyone, but after years of anger, sorrow and depression, I hadn't felt this good in such a long time.

I was feeling back to my old self, smiling, saying hello to everyone, and it seemed like a new world. A better world. I began a conversation with the woman in line behind me, as we were checking out. She was so positive, so happy, and we talked like we were old friends. By the time I checked out and loaded everything into my car, I was feeling like I was on a cloud. Life was feeling good.

I rushed home to Lizzie. I had left her at home, and told her not to move until I returned. I put away all the groceries, made her a snack, and went out on the patio to water the plants. I noticed a young woman, sitting out on the grass, at the end of the building. Her big brown Labrador Retriever was lying at her feet. It looked like she was getting some sun on her skin. I went inside to get more water, and when I came back outside, I noticed the woman had her head in her hands, like she was upset.

I sat down, and thought I would enjoy the fresh air for a little while. I was looking at my phone, reading emails, checking messages, and she was still there, still holding her head, still looking upset. I wanted to ask her if she was okay, but didn't know if she would appreciate the intrusion. Something inside kept pulling at me, nudging me to approach her.

I decided I couldn't take it anymore. I grabbed my sunglasses, told Lizzie I'd be right back, and walked outside. I walked over to her, and asked, "Are you okay?" She jumped up quickly, wiped her eyes, and said she was alright, she was just going through some stuff. She quickly added, it was a divorce.

"Oh, I've had two, I know it's hard," I told her.

She continued, "I was married for thirteen years, and my oldest daughter decided to go live with him, and she despises me now."

What?

Are you kidding? I couldn't believe this. Married thirteen years, daughter goes to live with dad, and suddenly hates her mom. I think I know this story, very well.

We spoke for a few minutes, introducing ourselves, and agreed that we needed to talk again one day, soon. It was unbelievable. I went back up to our apartment, and sat there, in disbelief. What are the chances? What are the chances that I just met someone with the same situation as mine, and at the same time God is working in my life? I think pretty slim.

I knew at this moment, I was supposed to meet her, and supposed to help in some way. Maybe meeting her was meant to comfort me, as well. Knowing God was making all of this happen was more than comforting.

I looked at Facebook shortly after this, that evening, and one of my friends had posted a picture, that read, "Those who put everything in God's hand will eventually see God's hand in everything." Yes, I agreed, and pretty quickly! I couldn't believe the timing.

I was so excited, I couldn't wait to see what was in store for me now. I had never, ever been excited about the future, not even when I was young. To feel this good, this "light," and free, and to know now that God was doing all of these things to show me He was there, and loves me, it was more than I deserved. I had been so horrible, so miserable, so ungrateful, and now look at all the love God was showing me.

The experience of knowing my aunt was with me, months before, when she communicated through my friend, had been nagging at me. Many times before, I had wanted to share it with my cousin, the daughter of that aunt. I was always hesitant, I wasn't quite sure how she would respond, knowing how others in my family had reacted. When I shared these experiences in the past, the reactions I received were those of great skepticism, I had felt judged and it made me uncomfortable.

Something told me now, that I needed to call her, I needed to share this with her. I sent her a text message telling her to call me when she had a minute, I had something to tell her, and that everything was good. She immediately called me. I explained that I had an experience that I felt I needed to share with her, something that had happened months ago, but I didn't know how she would take the news. I told her exactly the way it happened, with my friend who had dementia, and that I knew her mom had been there with me that day.

I was so relieved, she seemed pleased to hear the news, and even went a step further, and told me she had prayed I would one day talk about God with her. I told her what was going on in my life, and she recommended another show, a man she loved to watch. We had the most wonderful talk, and it felt so nice to really bond with her like this.

The minute I hung up the phone, I looked through the guide on television, found the show she had mentioned, and set the DVR once again to record. It would be recorded early the next morning.

I woke up the next day, made the coffee, and sat down to watch the show. During the first couple of minutes, he mentioned that when things are taken from us, even children, it's not God's work. God doesn't take children away, doesn't steal them. The devil takes children.

He said, John 10:10, "The thief comes only to steal and kill and destroy; I have come that they may have life, and have it to the full."

I sat there, sort of paralyzed for a few minutes, in disbelief over the timing. I couldn't believe my cousin had told me to watch this guy only the day before, and he's now talking about having a child taken, in the first couple of minutes of the show! I don't think this was an accident, there is no way this could be an accident, or just a coincidence. What are the chances that I had chose the day before to call my cousin, and she just happens to recommend a show, that in the first two minutes he changes my world?

I had thought for years that I was being punished, that God was so angry at me that He had taken Hannah away from me. All the people I had cut out of my life, because they couldn't help me get her back. All the years of watching the world keep going when I wanted to scream "Stop, don't you see what is happening?" "My child has been taken!" This injustice was being committed, my girls and I were all being ripped apart, and I was angry at the world. All the years of torment, anguish, depression, anxiety, so many years of pain, and I had thought I was being punished, punished by God.

I immediately sent a text message to my cousin, told her what had happened, and thanked her. She told me she loves it when things like that happen. Me, too. Me, too.

What a gift, what peace I was feeling. Another enormous weight lifted from my shoulders. More gratitude. More love. It was overwhelming, such a wonderful kind of overwhelming.

I truly was seeing God's hand in everything.

Yes. Just Yes.

Chapter 20

Thirty-three years ago, sitting in a funeral home, at the funeral of my good friend Mark, I was thinking all kinds of negative thoughts about myself. I wasn't normal, there was something wrong with me, I had some kind of "death vision." I was morbid. I was worthless. I was a worthless, morbid, psychic. I was in a fight with my friend who was now gone forever, I knew that day what a horrible person I was. If only I had a chance to talk to him, and make up the day before, when he had tried to find me. Filled with guilt, for over thirty years.

Again with Maggie, just two years after Mark's passing, look how terrible I was. Fighting, fighting, fighting, over something so stupid, and I would never get a chance to make peace with her. More guilt, more shame. That night, seeing her with the pink "glow" all around her, and wanting to apologize, but didn't. I missed my chance. I blew it off. Guilt.

I became so preoccupied with all of the weirdness, that I don't think I was really even fully "present" for a long time. It consumed my thoughts, and made me feel even more different than everyone else, even more wrong. I was just floating through the days, it felt, not really attached to my own life.

I had failed out of high school, and had collected all the guilt and shame from knowing what a complete disappointment I was.

I had let someone completely take advantage of

me, in such a filthy way, I felt so much shame and humiliation, and more guilt. I had no self-worth, and the self-loathing was growing.

If only I could go back in time, and grab that young girl I was, and tell her all the good news I was learning now, how much God really loves her, I wonder how her life would be today?

I thought about that young girl sitting at Young Life camp in Colorado, awkward in her own skin, feeling the pressure of the world, feeling pressure to ask Jesus into her heart. I would give anything to be able to go back and tell her what a wonderful thing she's doing! If only I could explain to her, that it's not just words, that she is actually setting herself up for the greatest life possible, if only I could tell her. If I could explain it all to her, maybe she would know she is loved, and she has worth, a future, hope, a strong foundation.

We can't build anything without a foundation. If you build a house, you start with a foundation, or a relationship, you have to have a foundation or it can't last. How can we expect our children, or anyone, to get through this life, with it's curve balls, storms, tragedies, injustices, whatever comes at us, without a foundation?

I was not raised in a church, or a religion, or any faith, really. I was raised on a foundation of "We're a family," and "We love each other no matter what." The Ten Commandments were the only kind of religion we had, and they really weren't discussed. We knew not to kill, cheat, or steal. My parents were good people, and I had a good family. I always thought family was everything. Families are wonderful.

Families fall apart every day. Families are destroyed overnight. Families are abandoned, and ripped to shreds.

I was starting to realize that God does not fall apart. God won't abandon you, and won't rip you to shreds. God doesn't fail. God doesn't lie, or cheat. God doesn't promise you everything, and then take it all away because He gets mad at you, or because He can't commit. God doesn't punish you by taking children away. God really does love you, and He gives you everything you need, love, courage, strength, wisdom, peace, and forgiveness, and more. Our lives are predestined, and with all of the gifts God gives us, why would anyone want to do life without Him? If I hadn't felt Him helping me, healing me, I probably wouldn't have ever believed that I could actually know God like this. He is there for you.

I had now learned so much, and I was still at the very beginning. I've started to look at life as an enormous platform, high up off the ground, with people on top going about their lives. There are storms, storms that blow up and try to knock all of the people off. Some get knocked off really quickly, all the way to the ground. Others are fighting, and fighting to stay on the platform, and just as they are knocked off they grab on to the side, and are hanging, clinging to the edge.

The storms are still blowing hard, but there are people still on the platform, kneeling down, and holding on, riding the storm. These are the people I have always wondered, "How do they have this peace about them, when all of these horrible things are happening?" "Why don't they struggle like I struggle?" You've seen them, during a tragedy, hardship, or a death, and they have this calm about them, and you're over here falling apart, feeling like the world is ending.

It might sound a little simplistic, but I have seen all of these people in my life, and watched as they struggled, including myself, struggled to get back on top of the platform. The people on the ground become so tired of making that climb back up to the top, that after a while, they begin to think it's too much work. They resort to "help," like drugs, alcohol, all the things that actually keep them on the ground, but they believe these things are helping. The people hanging on to the edge are the people "getting by" in life, just putting on a good face, getting through life, trying to make it to the end without "losing it."

Those people kneeling on the platform, they know they have real help. They know they are going to make it, and don't waste all of their energy fighting these storms, because they know with certainty, it will pass. They know God is there helping them, and He is going to get them through. They know they can do anything.

I have seen people like this my entire life, and always wanted what they have, that "knowing," that strength, but I could never figure out how to get it. It was right there, right in front of me the whole time, I just didn't have the knowledge, the education I needed to understand. I've always been hanging from the edge, and fallen off completely many times. Have you ever felt this way? When I was younger, I could usually climb back up on the platform. I was a survivor. I could always find some way to keep going. As I've gotten older, I haven't had any strength to come out on top anymore. It's not exactly a great way to live, it's not living at all. Now I feel strength and hope, thanks to God. Once you feel it, it's like magic.

It is like magic, how drastically everything in your life can change, as it did for me. It's a feeling you do not ever want to lose. The best part of it all, is that this is just the beginning. I know there is much more to come, and having a feeling a hope, not just "hope it works out," or "hope it's not going to be the worst," but hope in a sense of "I know it's going to be alright." It feels as if God picked me up, set me back on top of the platform, and said "I got you." This is literally how I feel, "lifted up," and loved. I have heard people say that, or pray that God would lift someone up, but to actually feel this? Truly indescribable. I could never do it justice with words.

I wanted so badly to go back and teach my children what I had just learned. I wanted them to have this knowledge, these tools for life. Look what has happened to my children, they have suffered through divorces, and having their foundation ripped out from under them.

What have I done?

I did the same thing to them that I had been taught. I gave them the same foundation of "family" that I had been given, and it has failed all of us. Knowing I caused them pain, suffering, it was unbearable. I caught myself slipping back into all of this negativity, guilt, and somehow it was short-lived, and used as a lesson for me. A lesson in self-forgiveness, which now I was realizing was just as important as forgiving others. It's crucial. God knows what is in your heart, and He knows your true spirit. I stopped beating myself up again for things I had done, because I hadn't had the knowledge I would have needed to change anything.

I would write more and more, and know that this is what I was supposed to do at the moment. It was healing me on the inside, teaching me, and I would pray constantly for God to let my girls feel His love and presence.

Lizzie couldn't help but soak up some of this new knowledge I was obtaining, because a lot of it was posted on notes around the house, and written all over the mirror in the bathroom. You couldn't leave the house now, without seeing the Lord's Prayer on the door, and a big note saying "Trust God." Every time I was leaving home, it would shift my focus for the day. It gave me energy to face whatever I had to face out there in the world. For someone who had basically been in almost complete seclusion, this was a drastic and healthy change.

Lizzie, I was determined, would not end up like me. She would know she could get through life knowing she was loved, and had a purpose, and would have the education she needed to weather any storm. She would have a relationship with God.

I knew she had mixed feelings about going to church, because Ron had taken her a few times, but forced her to sing, and threatened her if she didn't. She would tell me how uncomfortable she had been at these different churches with him, and when Chris and I would tell her we were going to church, she would never want to go.

We took her a few times, and reassured her she didn't have to sing, telling her it wasn't the kind of church that forced you to sing. Nobody should be that uncomfortable in church, it shouldn't be an unpleasant experience, especially for children!

I wanted her to know, it wasn't about the church, it wasn't about a certain denomination, it was about her relationship with God. I wanted her to want it on her own. I was relieved when she told me she understood, and knew the difference. We began to have the most wonderful conversations about God, and His plan, and how believing in and trusting God could make such an enormous difference in her life. I can't tell you how much this meant to me, for my daughter, at twelve, to have this understanding, something I wish I had known at her age. I had spent so much time worrying about my daughters experiencing some of the worst things that I had been through in my youth, and how these things could change who they were supposed to be. It was terrifying. I felt so much comfort now, knowing Lizzie knew these things already. Lizzie, at twelve, had already been through so much, but she had a healthy perspective and knew God would always be with her. I was grateful.

I had new hope for Rachel and Hannah, as well, even though I had failed both of them, I knew God would not, He would be with them. He had always been with me, I just didn't know it. More importantly, if He was with me, as awful as I had been, I was certain He was with my girls.

Gratitude. Lots of Gratitude.

Yes. Just Yes.

Chapter 21

It's truly a great day, when you can honestly say your anxiety is almost completely gone, and the depression you were suffering for years is completely gone. To feel peace for the first time in years, an unbelievable feeling. For a lot of people, it's probably pretty hard to believe, because so many people have to take a pill for anxiety, a pill for depression, and peace. So many people use alcohol and drugs to cope with all kinds of afflictions. I don't want to in any way offend anyone, not one person, who has to take any kind of medication for these afflictions. I, personally, have always been afraid of taking medication for my anxiety and depression, because I saw what effects they had on people I knew. Frankly, I can't even take a strong pain pill without experiencing scary side effects.

My purpose is truly only to tell my story, and honestly, I was shocked at how fast my depression disappeared! I had refused to see a doctor because I was afraid. Afraid of the medicine, afraid of admitting I was as bad as I was. I was trying so hard to act "normal."

I can tell you in all honesty, that having Hannah taken away like she was, almost killed me. You can actually die from a broken heart, and I felt like mine was killing me. I suffered for many years, and had terrible anxiety that would literally take over every aspect of my life. It was so horrible for a while I couldn't really get out of bed if Lizzie wasn't there. If she was home, I was with her, and would be a mom, and take care of her and her needs. She was my whole life. If she was gone, especially for weeks during the summer, I would fall apart, lose all of my energy, and go to a really dark, negative place. Lizzie was my purpose every day, and without her I was lost. I was paralyzed.

I would watch sad, horrible crime shows, grieve, cry, be miserable. This was where I was comfortable, as I've stated before. I could only focus on what I had lost, what was wrong, how all of these terrible things were happening to me.

It was a dark, sad place to be.

My anger was my weapon, I thought, against anyone who had hurt me, and especially anyone who wasn't helping me or feeling the pain over Hannah. I hadn't realized until now, how that anger was actually poisoning me little by little, stealing any joy I had. My anger, my hurt, and my fear were killing all of my happiness, and all of my relationships.

When I was crying out to God, and telling him how sorry I was for how awful I had been, it wasn't instant, but pretty close to it, he gave me a peace I had never known. It had now been a little over a month, or so, and every day had been getting better and better. I had so many revelations, about so many things. My days were spent doing basically the same thing every day, taking care of Lizzie, writing, studying, and going back through my life and thinking about all of my seemingly bizarre experiences.

All of the experiences when I thought I was "psychic," not knowing what else to call it, all of these memories were coming back for me to re-examine. The daydream I had when Mark died, and the experience when Maggie died, even "seeing" something on Ron's dad's face just moments before he passed away, and the dying cow, all of these times there was "something wrong" with me.

The time Jane was in a wreck, and I had felt such a strong feeling that I needed to drive her to Houston. The day of my sister's accident, the way I actually felt it inside of me that it was her, even though none of us could actually see the accident. All of these memories were now pouring through my mind.

I knew with certainty at this point that I wasn't psychic, and that I had always known there was a God, I just hadn't put it all together, until now. For the first time I could really believe, one hundred percent, God had been with me, all along. From that first night at camp in Colorado when I asked Jesus into my heart, just to please everyone, I thought. That night, over thirty years ago, changed my life.

He had been there all along, guiding me, and I had fought it throughout my life. I didn't know what I was doing. That "knowing" I had during times of tragedy, or death, was Him. He had tried to get through to me so many times, and I was so stubborn, and couldn't believe. I truly think He was guiding me the day of my sister's accident so my mother, and my sister's children would have the help they needed. Those were the actions He guided me to take, to be there for them. He used me for a purpose. He was there, with me.

I knew that night that when Faith appeared out of nowhere, out of the dark, to help me. God was guiding her, as well. I felt it that night, I just didn't really believe it, I thought it was like a "one-time" thing. I assumed there could not have been any other explanation for what happened, but knowing now that it *was* God, I believe it. Not only do I believe it, I know it! What other explanation can anyone find for this many "coincidences," this many perfectly intersecting actions of so many people? When I felt it, I knew instinctively that it was God, and now I know that I had been right.

I had that part right, but I was missing the other part, the ability to handle everything that was happening. If I had the knowledge then, that I have now, I think I could have been more helpful to everyone. I would have been able to help my sister, and my mother, in the months after the accident, without it taking all of my energy. I didn't know any better, and I did my best, but it wasn't much of an effort, I admit. I wouldn't have let the whole experience start killing my soul. After the death of my dad, and then the accident that ended the life of my little nephew, the sadness and grief was too much for me to handle. I was falling apart, falling off the platform.

I didn't have the knowledge, the foundation, to know that I could have faith, strength, courage, and make it through the enormous storms, and help others through, as well. I always wanted to believe that sweet little baby boy was with my dad, on the other side, up in Heaven, whatever the other side was. I needed to believe this was the truth, but I had so much doubt. It was just too sad, too much to bear.

That time in our lives is what ripped our family completely apart. If we had a foundation, if we had faith, we might have stayed together as a family, and not been split down the middle. I know it's hindsight, but I truly believe at the very least, our family needed some type of faith. Without faith, or any relationship with God, you can look up one day and realize you don't really have anything, you don't even have a family.

I began to wonder why I was adopted into this family, if I was destined to know God, and have a relationship with Him. Why would He put me with a family that didn't practice religion? My parents had been raised in different denominations, and were very good people, but we didn't really practice any religion. I had ruined our one chance at going to church as a family, I thought, by contracting the Mumps. Why was I placed in the family that adopted me if this was my destiny? I love my family, but I was questioning everything.

I had no chance of having God in my life, or learning the Bible as a child, and I think He knew this. I thought about it for a while, a long time, and I became convinced that God had guided me to the right place, the right time, and gave me the opportunity to find Him. Somehow I made my way to that camp, the camp I wasn't even sure I wanted to attend, but I made it there. That camp was the whole reason I am where I am today. I wish He had done something about that crazy horse I got stuck with, but I am still very grateful I had been at that camp, at that time in my life. The whole experience doesn't seem so bad now, if all I had to do was get bucked off a horse and have the seat of my pants rip in front of everyone, and rappel off the side of a cliff. Look at what I have received in return. God has been with me, throughout my life.

He was there through all of those hard times, really sad times, and I thought, how awesome God is! I wasn't an Angel of Death, I was a child of God. I wasn't a psychic, God was there preparing me, guiding me through tragic times. Everything was falling into place, every little doubt I ever had, getting erased. Every memory I had was now becoming easier to remember, without emotions and guilt tagging along.

Gratitude. Lots of gratitude.

Yes. Just Yes.

Chapter 22

So here we are, the part I have been a little nervous about writing, the part about the devil. I don't know about you, but as a child, I was afraid of talking about the devil, or saying the word Satan, because that is what the really "religious" people did. That's just how it was. I heard things like you shouldn't be a "Bible beater," or a "Jesus freak," and you don't go around talking about Satan. I grew up hearing about the devil from others, and until recently, never liked saying that word. I never really thought it was a "real" thing. I knew there was God, and I knew about Jesus, but to say that other word, was just not in my vocabulary. I knew there was evil, but I thought only evil people did evil things.

When my cousin had recommended the show she liked I had watched it, and in the first couple of minutes the pastor said that having a child taken is the devil's work. I was so relieved. Relieved because I thought I was being punished by God, and that's why she was taken away from me.

It was the devil's work. The devil. So hard for me to accept, because I never really thought it was real. A friend had been telling me that the devil puts all the negative thoughts in your head, and you tell him to go away, in "Jesus' name." After she told me that, I heard Joyce Meyer say the same thing. Still, not quite convinced, another friend, Meredith reiterated what they had said. I know it sounds silly, but this is how I felt. I had been taught throughout my life to think only weirdo's went around saying these kinds of things. It felt so awkward to say these words!

1 Peter 5:8 "Be alert and of sober mind. Your enemy the devil prowls around like a roaring lion looking for someone to devour."

The devil is literally prowling around, and the closer you get to God, the more he attacks, tries to convince you that you aren't good enough, you can't do something, you have committed the worst sins, or you are just bad. I think this was one of the toughest things I had to accept, but once I did, it made so many other things make sense, finally. I felt like I was being attacked more and more over the last few weeks, and both of my friends that were aware of what was happening, said it was because I was getting so close to God. God was working in my life, and any little opportunity the devil had, he would literally tell me I wasn't good enough, or I was a horrible person, a failure, worthless, or this or that.

I began to do what everyone said to do, tell him to leave me alone, in Jesus' name. I felt a little crazy doing this at first, but when I realized it was working, I felt this peace again, and it was done. I was on my way now to an incredible place, where I could actually get that anxiety, those self-loathing thoughts completely out of my head, by saying a few words, very powerful words! Those thoughts had kept me down for so many years.

I thought of Hannah, and how all the times I had felt, and heard in my head, that I had been a bad mother, and God was punishing me by taking her. I thought about when she had first told me she was leaving to go live with her dad, and how I was reacting so badly. I was out of control, but these thoughts were going through my head, thoughts I know now were the enemy. It was constant, the self-doubt, the self-loathing, the awful and overwhelming, paralyzing fear.

Thoughts that everyone knew something I didn't know, something people thought I had done, but hadn't. I felt like all the mothers of Hannah's friends were judging me, like everyone was judging me, and I had no idea why, or what I had done. I always felt like people viewed me as some type of criminal, and I felt like I was being treated like one. I know a couple of those women had tried to help me keep her, and I appreciated their help, but I still felt the judgment, real or imagined. It was absolutely crazy all the thoughts and emotions I was going through. The truth is, it was all a distraction, so that I wouldn't know how to fight her leaving. I would be so paralyzed, that I wouldn't be able to stand up and fight for my child.

I kept saying the whole time it was happening, that it didn't feel like a fair fight, that I was losing before the battle even began. I guess when you are fighting evil, that's how it feels, because that's exactly what I went through. I wish I had known, I wish I had known how to fight the devil off back then. Even if I had still lost Hannah, I would have given it a shot, given all I had with strength, tools and wisdom. I would have at least been able to protect my girls a little more, and protect myself. It's hurt all three of my girls, having their sisters ripped apart, and it almost destroyed me completely.

My sweet daughter, caught up in this evil, and it happened right in front of everyone. It seemed as though nobody could stop it. I had always been so full of fear, under control, and trained to be afraid to divorce my husband. Threatened, if I divorced him, that he would take my kids away.

I look back now, and I can't even figure out when it began, that fear. Why in the world was I so afraid? I had always felt so powerless in that marriage, and I had no voice, but how could I have been terrified of divorcing him, and having my children taken? I wasn't doing anything to deserve losing a child, I knew I wasn't a criminal. I was a mother. I took care of my children. I was accused of holding them too much when they were infants, and accused of being over-protective. My babies were clean, fed, healthy and loved. As they got older, I helped them with school projects, baked cupcakes, carted them around to all of their activities and appointments, took care of them when they were ill. The list goes on and on. I was doing what mothers do. I wasn't a spectacular mother, but I certainly wasn't a bad mother. Why was I so afraid?

It was so gradual, I guess, there was a conditioning that I didn't notice until it was too late. I always thought of my marriage like the boiling frog story. The story of when you put a frog in a pot of water, slowly turn the heat up in such small increments that he doesn't even notice when the water is boiling, and doesn't hop out. The frog dies. I think that is exactly how the devil works. Gradually. Prowling. That word keeps going through my mind. A prowling predator. That's how I felt, like I could never really have peace, because there was a prowling predator, going to take my children. I had to be careful of what I did or said. That is not a marriage.

Knowing now that this was the devil's work, at least I could tell Lizzie and Rachel what I've realized, and they can learn to fight the evil out of their own lives. I was determined to make something positive out of what has happened to me, and my innocent children.

I still feel a little strange saying "the devil," and especially Satan, but honestly, since I know I've experienced plenty of the poison in my own mind, for years and years, I can at least say it. That's all he is, poison. You don't have to drink it. You don't have to listen to it. God is all about love, peace, and forgiveness. You are His child, and you have to fight off the enemy and not let him steal any of your joy and happiness, or your worth. We are to fight evil with love.

I've listened to the enemy for too long, he kept me stuck in a dark place, kept me from moving forward, kept me from enjoying life. He's there, always, waiting to poison your mind and tell you that you can't do something. I have felt like I've been under attack for a long time, but never so much as this time I have been getting so close to God, here recently in these last few weeks. Since the day I had my "meltdown," and God picked me up, and has been showing me so much love, I have been attacked all day, every day. It's been constant.

When I started writing, it became worse, and I literally have had to tell him to leave me alone at least a dozen times a day. I know, to some of you, you might think this sounds ridiculous, and I would have thought the same way a long time ago. But not anymore. I've felt it, experienced it, and I know it's very real. This is the only way I learn anything in life, I have to experience it, feel it for myself, and I'm pretty sure that's why it has taken me fifty years to get here.

All the negativity is the enemy. As I would write, those old thoughts of "You can't write, you failed English in high school" and "You aren't smart enough to write a book." I would hear over and over, "You're not a good person, look at your sins." These are just the nicest examples I can give, there are much worse, but I've learned to fight it off, fight off the poison. There have been a few times I didn't fight, the times I was actually the most relaxed, most at peace, and the enemy would start to get into my head. Now that I have these tools, and this knowledge, I don't really worry about what he says, and best of all, I have no more fear.

When you realize how real the enemy is, you can then look back on your life, and not feel so much guilt. This was happening to me, almost daily. It's all a process, I think, that is healthy to go through, but not dwell in for too long. I think it might help all of us to know we don't need to feel so much guilt for all of the horrible things that have happened in our past, especially if you've been violated in some way.

So many people feel like they are to blame for such awful things that have happened to them, even when they are innocent victims. I can't tell you how many times I thought about things that happened to me as a teenager, getting violated, and still thinking somehow I did something to cause it to happen. Why? Why do we do this to ourselves? I didn't do anything about it, because I thought it was my fault, and was so worried about other people blaming me. That's exactly what the enemy wants you to think! I know I'm not alone, and if I can reach one person and help them free themselves of that self-destructive guilt, then it's a good day.

To know that the devil is real, and maybe sometimes an excuse for why people do hurtful things, can take that victim's guilt away, through God's love. This is what has helped me, I think, forgive the truly awful offenses against me. If you can get to that point, and truly forgive the most horrible actions of others, it will bring you such peace, and free your soul. You also must forgive yourself, for any hurt and harm you have caused. This gives you an amazing power to move forward with nothing but positive thoughts, leading to positive living, which is exactly what God wants.

I never understood how that worked before, and I am truly grateful I understand it now. To really get it, you must understand that the devil is real. He's always there, prowling, ready to strike, ready to bring you down. If you know how to fight him off, you can only increase your happiness, your peace, your strength. If it feels awkward or unbelievable to you, trust me, I understand. It felt that way for me, at first, but once you see results, you'll never doubt again.

I've learned to fight off the fear, as well. I now pray for the enemy, which I've said before, I never thought I would do. I'm not saying I'm fantastic at praying for the enemy, but I'm doing it.

Ephesians 6:11 "Put on the full armor of God, so that you can take your stand against the devil's schemes."

Peace. So much peace.

Gratitude. So much gratitude.

Yes. Just Yes.

Chapter 23

Weeks have passed since Lizzie's surgery, and she is recovering very well. She has now even started going to school for a couple of hours here and there, and is acclimating back into the busy day. Her recovery has been for the most part just as the doctor told us it would be. No real surprises, thank God. These weeks at home for us have been healing on so many different levels, her body is healing, and her mom is healing. The atmosphere in our home was always one of peace and comfort, but now even more peace, and it's even more comfortable. There is a new feeling in the air. Lizzie's teacher, Diana, had paid us the most wonderful compliment, she told us our home was her favorite home to visit, and not just because of the wonderful coffee! It really made me feel good, to know she felt the peace in our home that I felt.

I was still missing Chris, and trying to figure out what was going on in his mind. I had a feeling I knew, but I really wasn't sure. All I could do was pray for him, pray for God to bring him back to me, pray for God to do what he thought was best. One night, late at night, I was just about to fall asleep, when I heard my phone ring. I knew in my heart it was Chris. I looked at the screen, and saw it was him.

We talked, and talked, and ended up on the phone for almost four hours. It was so wonderful to hear his voice, and he sounded alright, but not great. He told me I sounded good. We talked and laughed about so many different things. It was comforting. When we hung up, finally, I thanked God for this gift I had received, this wonderful, wonderful gift.

I had told Chris that we had taken Lizzie to see a movie, and he quickly asked "Who's we?" It sounded like he was a little jealous, until I told him it had been Rachel and I that had taken Lizzie out for a movie. As small as it was, it was a little glimmer of hope for my heart, maybe he still cared. He called me "Babe" a few times. I didn't know if it was out of habit, or on purpose, but it also gave me more hope. I tried not to get my hopes up too high, but I couldn't help myself, falling into the familiar feelings of love for him.

The next day we talked a little more, and texted for the next couple of days after that. The next call went a little weird, a little negative, and I had a bad feeling. Our text messages weren't any better.

I went back over everything in my mind, and remembered everything we talked about, everything he said. I had told him I was close with God, and he told me he had lost that closeness, and couldn't get it back. That really stuck in my head, he couldn't get back to God.

During this time of communicating with him, I completely lost focus on my writing, and couldn't finish a chapter. I felt a sense of panic, which turned into a little bit of fear. Pretty soon I was experiencing a bit of anxiety.

What was happening to me? I couldn't get focused. I was starting to get a little nervous, everything had been so even and peaceful before these last few days. All of the sudden, things went south, and fast. Chris was back to ignoring me. It only took a few short days.

I could not understand what was going on. I thought God had put us together in the first place. I knew we were supposed to be together, in some capacity. I knew it, even if we were only to be friends. I knew he loved me and my girls, or at least he told me he did. What in the world happened? I was so confused. I was also completely distracted from the book, and not even working on it for a day or two. I went back to my little composition book full of prayers and Bible verses, and I prayed harder. I had somehow jumped the track, and was desperately trying to climb back up. I couldn't believe I was losing everything. Not this, don't lose this! I prayed, asked God to get me back on track, back to what He wanted me to write. I tried to stay busy.

After a day or two, everything went back to my "new" normal, I was so relieved to be back in my peaceful place, and felt like I could write again. It was like a switch had been flipped, literally that fast.

I sat down and wrote another chapter, and it just flowed right out of me, and into my laptop. My peace of mind was back. No fear, no anxiety, I wasn't worried about anything, especially not Chris.

I finally realized, it was the enemy. Chris was letting the devil put negative thoughts in his head. The difference in our first conversation and the last, was just as contradictory as good and evil. It made perfect sense. I was getting sucked back into that dark place, because Chris was there. He wasn't fighting it off. Meredith, and another friend had both told me, God rips people out of your life, sometimes temporarily, so He can spend time with you, and get close to you. This was a crazy notion to me at first, but honestly, it felt like that was exactly what was happening.

If Chris hadn't been gone out of my life right now, I wouldn't have experienced any of these wonderful things. I don't think I would have even started this book, or almost be finished with the book. My first book. I wouldn't have this close relationship with God, and wouldn't be learning all of these valuable things. I most likely wouldn't have had the healing, either, if Chris had still been here. The healing I had needed for so many years.

All of these truly amazing things wouldn't be happening in my life, none of them, probably, because I would be distracted, and focused on the wrong things. If I had to choose between my new life without all of the depression, anger, anxiety and being totally lost, or Chris, there was no question, I'd go without Chris! It was not a tough decision, it just still hurt how everything had happened the way it did.

It was sad for me to realize, because I loved Chris, but right now, for all of these different reasons, he needed to remain absent. I had such a hard time accepting my behavior, knowing I had told him to get out of my life, but I thought it was because I was in such horrible shape at the hospital. I was experiencing so much trauma seeing Lizzie like she was, not sleeping at all, I had been sick, all of these things going on, I just wasn't myself at all. He had been angry, frustrated, and had taken it out on me, when I barely had any strength to get through a day. I had acted out of fear, and sheer delusion. Now I was wondering, if, in fact, this was all part of God's plan.

It was confusing, because everything I was reading and hearing, was "never give up on anyone," and "love never fails," or "love perseveres," yet the door to Chris was shut and locked! How do you know when it's God's plan, or whether or not you should keep trying?

Ephesians 2:10 "For we are God's (own) handiwork (His workmanship), recreated in Christ Jesus, (born anew) that we may do those good works which God predestined (planned beforehand) for us (taking paths which He prepared ahead of time), that we should walk in them (living the good life which He prearranged and made ready for us to live)."

God's plan. Predestined. How do we know what that is? How do I not follow my instincts, or follow my heart, or follow God's plan, how do I know the difference?

It was becoming more confusing the more I read. The more I studied, the more confused I became. I finally had no choice but to let go, let go of everything and trust God. I admit, I am stubborn, but when you have lived your life feeling so powerless, to let go and trust completely feels like jumping from a cliff. I would have to go about my life, my days, doing what I needed to do, and just trust Him. He was, after all, already guiding me. Just relax. Live. Trust.

Trust. The hardest thing in the world for me to do. I had never been able to truly trust anyone after my two failed marriages. I'm not sure I ever trusted anyone completely in my entire life. It was difficult. I had been suspicious of everyone, even people I had no reason to suspect of anything, I was still suspicious. I even told Chris when I first met him, I don't trust, I have trust issues. I warned him. He always said, "You get punched in the nose too many times, you learn you can't trust."

I knew he had his own trust issues, but somehow we always worked through things, even the worst things. It was not a perfect relationship, but it was the first relationship I ever had that involved any communication. Seriously, simple communication, it was a first for me, and it wasn't even that great. In my marriages, I felt like I was talking to the wall. In my second marriage, even when I was asked to give an opinion it was "wrong." When there is no communication, you feel like you have no worth in a relationship, and you feel like you have nothing to trust, how nice would it be to know you could trust God?

Knowing now that God already knows everything that will happen to me, and that He knows what's best, how could I insult Him and not trust Him? I couldn't insult Him after everything He was doing for me.

I have to admit, I had fought even the simplest things about my new relationship with God. At first, I had a really hard time even thinking of Him as my Father. My dad was such a good man, such a good father, and I still missed him every single day, and he had been gone over twelve years now. To call God my Father, at first, I felt like I was somehow being disloyal to my dad.

I know that might sound silly, or stupid. If you understand how this whole "language" was looked upon in my childhood, you'd understand. It wasn't just people in my family, but other people in our lives, it was simply how people around me thought of religion. Because of this influence, I always felt awkward with the language, and it was tough to fight it off. I was changing drastically now, my thoughts, my heart, my soul, my language, everything was changing.

It seemed like the people I was interacting with at this time were so comfortable in this new language I was learning, it made it easier to for me to adjust. It felt like God had put these people in my life for this reason. I was beginning to realize that God might have put Lizzie's teacher, Diana, and my friend Meredith, front and center in my life for a reason. They were there to help me in my transformation. The timing was too perfect, I thought, for there to be any other explanation.

The funniest thing to me, is that all this love God was showing me now, and all the times he has now let his presence be known in my little life, it's never been about my non-practicing religion. I believed in God, but my belief in Him was lacking real knowledge. I had been so terrified of religion my whole life, and part of the fear came from being around "religious" people. There were actually people telling me that their denomination was the "right" denomination, and the others were "wrong." One friend couldn't walk into another friend's church for a wedding, because something dreadful would happen to her. What? How does one choose a denomination, knowing there are right ones, and wrong ones? It was easier not to choose one at all, frankly, and this attitude only scares people away from any religion. This can't be what God wants. If there was a right one, how could He have found me, and helped me if I was so lost, and I wasn't any particular denomination? I ignored Him.

When Rachel was in the eighth grade, a woman that worked in the office at her school actually told my daughter she was going to hell, because she wasn't Baptized. It made me so angry, I almost went to the school to confront her. I've seen Christians treat people in their own family, and others, terribly, and then quote scripture like a champ. People who had true hardships, really sad things happen to them, they were judged and abandoned, by their own "religious" family.

When you see so much of this behavior from Christians, you don't exactly want to jump on the wagon. Everything they did was because of their "religion." They weren't loving people and helping people that needed help. All they were doing was condemning these people who honestly, were sometimes the victims of circumstances beyond their control. It is confusing when you believe in God, but then you're surrounded by all of the conflict between individual beliefs of different denominations.

It's not about other people's beliefs, and rules, at all. It's about God, and our personal relationship with Him. I am an average person, with an average life. I have no educated religion. Trust me, if He has spent this much time with me, He is bigger and more awesome than all of it. He's not worried about which church I've been to, or my brief existence as a Methodist! He loved me up even though I couldn't quote one single scripture. Not one! I believe it's more important to God that we actually live the scripture, and act it out, rather than only be able to quote the words.

I now had to learn how to trust, fully and completely, that God knew what was best for me. I had already felt like I had turned everything over to Him, and had already seen so many wonderful things happen, so quickly.

To say I could trust one hundred percent, I didn't really know if I could. After the whole experience with Chris, and how it ended so abruptly, and so badly, I knew I had absolutely no idea what I was doing. I had no idea what was happening, or what to think, and I truly wanted what was best for all of us, especially my girls.

I just kept saying over and over, "I trust you God, I trust you God," and I really wanted to mean it with all of my heart. I didn't want to try His patience, He had already been so good to me, when I didn't deserve it.

It seems like everywhere I looked, I saw something that said "Trust Him, He knows what He's doing," or even on my own bathroom mirror, where I wrote it myself, "God's plan is the best plan." I could do this. For once I had to trust completely. This was God, after all.

Matthew 22:17 "Love the Lord your God with all hour heart and with all your soul and with all your mind."

1 Corinthians 13:7 "(Love) It always protects,

always trusts, always hopes, always perseveres."

There it was. I had to trust, because love always trusts. I love God, and we are supposed to love Him with all of our hearts, souls, and minds.

I had to make a conscious decision to really let go of Chris, somehow. God was working in my life, he was also working in Chris's life, and as hard as it was, I had to do this. There they were, little notes that said "Let it go," popping up around the house. I felt this was a little ironic, after I had become so sick of the song "Let it go" from the children's movie "Frozen." I begged Lizzie to only listen to it when I wasn't around. I couldn't bear to hear it anymore, not one bit of it. I was now singing it, every time I glanced at one of the notes.

You've heard the saying, I'm sure, the one that says "When God shuts a door, stop knocking on it." Well, it's embarrassing, but I was always the one standing there banging on the closed door. Not only banging, but trying everything I could to knock the door down, or force it open. I was pitiful. I'm a "fixer." I feel like I have to fix everything. I have never been able to let things be. It goes against my nature to let things be. The temptation to call, or text Chris was always there. Always. This was going to be a real struggle.

Trust God.

Just as things had been happening, right on cue, I get a phone call, from an old friend. She was calling to ask how Lizzie was doing, and I hadn't talked to her since just after the surgery, now almost eight weeks ago. We talked for a while, about her kids, our lives, and somehow we started talking about God, of course.

It seemed like every conversation I was getting into lately, somehow always got around to God. I told her what was happening to me, and she immediately began to tell me the exact thing Chris had said to me during the last conversations I had with him.

She was also once close to God for about a year, but couldn't seem to get back to Him. I couldn't believe the parallels in the two conversations, with both of these people that I truly loved. It was shocking to hear her say these things, I always thought of her as such a strong spiritual person.

The words they both said were almost identical. They both told me to "run with it," my new bond with God, for they had both had it and lost it. I knew God was working at that moment, guiding me, guiding all of us. I told her about the shows I was watching, and the way I was studying, and told her to call me after she watched one of the shows. I wasn't really sure what else I was supposed to do, but I was certain God was working.

I certainly didn't want to lose what I had, and hearing both of their stories, I was determined to keep Him close. I didn't want to get off track again, like I had with Chris, who was in a dark and negative place, a place that was scary to me now. I was beginning to believe what my friends had said, that maybe he was "ripped" out of my life because God had something much better in mind.

It becomes much easier to trust Him, when He's showing you every day that He's right there, right in your life, and He knows I need those signs. He is so wonderful, so awesome, and my life is still changing daily. I would reflect back over just the previous couple of weeks, and see all the incredible things He was doing, it was overwhelming. I was truly in awe.

Gratitude.

Yes. Just Yes.

Chapter 24

I know some people might think that this is all too many rainbows, too many unicorns, and to tell you the truth, two months ago, I probably wouldn't have believed it, either. I get it. I don't even think I believed it at first when it was happening to me! I felt it, I could see it, but I couldn't believe it.

My purpose is not to tell anyone what to do, or what to believe, I know everyone is different, and experiences things differently. Some people can go to church, and read the Bible, and they are happy, they know who they are in Christ. I am not that kind of person. I have to experience everything to an extreme. I have to hit the wall sometimes three, even four times or so, before I can actually "get it." It's simply the way I'm wired.

I felt an urge to write my story for so long, not even knowing that this story was even possible. I could never figure out what I was supposed to write, but I knew I needed to write. God had put it on my heart so long ago, but I know now that I wasn't ready yet, my story hadn't happened until now. The beginnings were there, but it was still premature. I had to wait until now. I laugh, because I always struggled in my twenties, my thirties, even my forties, struggled to write, and who knew, a month after I turned fifty, my story would come to life! It truly is amazing, what God has done with my life. I feel so blessed, truly blessed, that He loves me enough to give me a purpose, and has given me such clarity.

He loves all of us this way, truly unconditionally. He wants us to live life to the fullest. He gives us everything we need to live a full, purposeful, happy life, and the love to help others. That is our purpose, I know now, to help others, and He gives us all different gifts to do so.

I could not have written one page a few months ago. I was in such horrible shape, there is no way I could have sat down and written even one little page. I would have gotten confused, angry, frustrated, and unsatisfied with anything I had written. It would not have been possible to write at all.

There was so much negativity in my life, and some of it I didn't even realize it was even there, until now. I think it had been building up for so many years, that now I really don't even recognize myself when I think back to that other person. I had tried so hard to change myself, for the longest time, and I continued to fall deeper and deeper into the darkness.

Chris had given it his best, as well. I woke up one morning while he was at the gym, and I found a note from him. It said he had a good plan for the day, nothing but good, positive energy, and a good plan. He tried so hard, and I always found a way to fight it. We did have really good times, and good days, but it was always my first instinct to fight it off.

There are so many little things today, just a few short weeks since my meltdown, that have either been wiped away, or changed completely.

The obvious things, like my paralyzing anxiety, my deep depression, my anger, they were noticeably gone right away. Fear. I had lived with so much fear. I'm not afraid of anything at all, now. Nothing, not even death. For me to say that, and I know my children will even tell you this is completely true, and I almost want to call it a miracle. My girls probably would classify this as a miracle, also, given the amount of my "paranoia" they had to live with growing up.

Poor Rachel called me after she went off to college one day, and was telling me about all of these exciting things she was doing. I sat there on the phone with her, and made sure I told her about everything horrible and scary that could happen, and told her to watch out for this or that, it was ridiculous. I honestly thought that if I said it out loud, it wouldn't happen. She finally asked me, "Mom, why does every scenario end in my death?" She had a point.

Look what I had done to my child! That's not healthy, to say the least. That is the world I lived in, scary, you lose your children, bad things happen, it went on and on. What a bitter pill I had to take, realizing I had been projecting all of that fear and darkness on my daughter. I was so happy for her when she was accepted into the university, and then I sat there and filled her with all of this horrible negativity. I was so embarrassed about my behavior. I had been honestly thinking the whole time that I was somehow protecting her from something bad happening to her.

Thank God, all of that fear is gone, and the behavior can be much more positive now, healthier for all of us. I no longer fear the future, which has always been a constant in my life. Now, when my head hits the pillow at night, the endless stream of frightening things happening to my girls isn't running through my head. It just doesn't happen anymore. This is such a drastic change, and I am extremely grateful for this beautiful gift. This gift alone is so wonderful, but God has for some reason given me so much more, much more than I deserve.

I would like to say that suddenly I am this unbelievably patient person, but that will take a little more time. I can say I do have more patience. I find myself driving much slower, and staying in the "slow" lane more often. I'm not really in much of a rush, and I'm not getting angry at other drivers at all. I have become that annoying driver that lets too many cars in front of them, and I feel good about it. This part I find particularly comforting, because I truly love to drive. Something I shared with my dad. Growing up in my family, you are taught to drive very early. By early, I mean by the age of ten you can drive cars, and even tractors. Driving is something I love, and it is almost therapeutic for me. It feels good to relax and enjoy the ride now, no matter where I am going.

No more guilt, no more sadness, and especially no more of the painful anxiety to keep me stuck in one spot. The poison I had been watching on television has now been replaced with good, wholesome, positive shows, if I watch any at all. There is no negativity anywhere in my home, my heart, my mind, it is just gone. Our home has always been full of love, but it has become such a peaceful place, even more than before, and you can feel it.

I've become very aware of negative things other people say, especially if they're talking about other people. I have this little reaction inside of me. I can't let any negativity enter my ears. It really bothers me. I have so much peace inside, I don't want to risk losing any of it. I think also, once you realize that God thinks of us as His children, you start to think differently about other people, even the people that have hurt you.

I know I have been so negative, and I don't know how my friends and family put up with me for so long. I was hearing how it sounded now, as I listened to people, constantly talking about negative things, and it does not feel very pleasant. I had talked incessantly about losing Hannah, to a few people in my life, because it was all I could think about most of the time. I always felt like someone could do something to fix it, someone could help, but I had to keep talking about it.

If you stop talking about people you've lost, people forget about them, right? Somehow I thought if I stopped talking about Hannah, people would accept the situation, and forget I had a beautiful daughter named Hannah, that was taken. I couldn't accept this, ever, I had to keep talking about her. My sadness had totally consumed me, and taken over almost every aspect of my life, preventing me from enjoying anything, really.

I don't think I've ever felt this level of contentment, or had this much peace. I really can't believe I was ever so low, and didn't realize how low I was until now. All the years of thinking I was worthless, and a failure, weighted down with guilt and shame. I would have never dreamed there was such a feeling of peace, and even if I did, I wouldn't have thought I could feel it.

I think the biggest change in my every day life at this point in my new journey is that I can now look at the pictures of Hannah around my home, without feeling anxiety or pain. I can look at her and smile. I look at her and remember cute things she said, sweet things she did, good, happy, positive memories. I can clean out a closet and stumble upon something of Hannah's, or go through the girl's handwork from when they were little, and not completely fall to pieces. I can miss her, but I don't have to be depressed anymore. I can miss her, but don't have to cry every single day that she's gone. I can think about the crime of her being taken, but I don't have to be taken over by thoughts of hate, feelings of bitterness, or fantasize about taking revenge.

I have spent years swimming around a dark hole, feeling all kinds of guilt, just stuck in the same grief every single day. All the years of depression, anxiety, heart break, pure anguish, they did not bring her back. Those things took my joy away, took so much of my happiness away, and the time is just lost. We can't ever get that time back with Hannah, not one single day out of over twenty-five hundred that we've lost. Over two thousand, five hundred days of pure torture.

I can now trust God, and pray to Him, that He protect her, and that He lets her feel His presence, and love, and hope that some day it's in God's plan that we all be reunited. Rachel, Lizzie, and Hannah, they are sisters, and there is no reason they should have been separated. I'm grateful I know now that it was the enemy, and I have the peace knowing I wasn't being punished, especially seeing the pain and maybe permanent damage it's caused my children.

Romans 12:2 "Do not conform to the pattern of this world, but be transformed by the renewing of your mind. Then you will be able to test and approve what God's will is – his good, pleasing and perfect will."

All of these changes, and all such positive changes, it's honestly like I have a whole new life, so much more than I deserve. In a few short weeks, I went from dark to peace, bitterness to forgiveness, anger and grief to contentment. God is awesome, He did this for me. He has changed my world.

So much gratitude.

Yes. Just Yes.

Chapter 25

Lizzie was on the mend, but still needed plenty of rest. She was attending school for a few hours, a few days a week. Not a full schedule yet, but we were getting there. Sitting in school for just a few hours made her back hurt, and just riding in the car, hitting bumps and holes, would still give her pain. She still needed a little help doing a few every day activities we all take for granted, but she had come so far. Just brushing her hair was an ordeal, it was long, and curly, and tangled easily. Every tangle caused her pain, and I would have to separate her hair into tiny sections just to gently brush them out. This was nothing compared to what we had already been through, and it seemed we could see the light at the end of the tunnel, finally.

Ron and his wife, and one of her sons came out to visit Lizzie one weekend. They played a game with her, and visited for about an hour. She seemed to enjoy the game, it was some sort of card game. She also seemed to enjoy the company.

A couple of weeks later, he called on one of his scheduled calls, which were twice a week, on the same days every week. He wanted to come get Lizzie and take her for visitation for the weekend. I had told her already, that since we couldn't feel what she was feeling, this decision would be up to her. I didn't want to push her, she had already pushed herself too far one day at school, stayed way too long, and had been in a lot of pain all day.

When he called, I gave her the phone, and left the room. After a few minutes, I went to see if she was off the phone, and saw her holding it up to her ear, and she had tears in her eyes.

What? I asked what was wrong, and she said he had told her no, he was coming to get her. She had tried multiple times to tell him she wasn't ready.

I took the phone from her, and thought I would explain she wasn't ready. He wouldn't have it. He went on and on, and said I was trying to keep him from his daughter.

What? Did you see what she went through at the hospital? Weren't you there? I was stunned. I had never tried to keep him from his children, but it had been done to me. He had just come to visit a couple of weeks before, I told him he was welcome to visit again. That did not work, either.

This was not making sense. She's twelve years old, and should have the right to decide this for herself, given what she had been through, I thought. He said he had talked to the doctor and they said she was fine, and could travel, and that she needed to get out and do more things. I explained how she went to school for too long and was in pain. I explained we didn't even get to go to my mom's for Thanksgiving, because Lizzie didn't want the hour long car ride, and the dirt road, full of bumps. He asked why I would go to my mom's anyway, because, he said, my mother doesn't even like me. Really? What in the world is happening?

I finally told him that Lizzie was twelve, and should be able to make the decision all by herself. Hannah, after all, was only a year or so older at the time he let her decide to move to live with him. He had the nerve to say, "But you never came to visit Hannah," said only to impress who I assume was sitting next to him, his new wife. She had no idea, I'm sure, of the hundreds of rejections I had experienced from Hannah, and the incredible amount of pain and anguish I endured over having her taken away. Not to mention, Lizzie and I gave up a wonderful life in Corpus Christi, and moved all the way up to Fort Worth for Hannah. The way he was speaking, the things he was saying, I knew she had been hand-fed the same information as the last wife.

Insults were thrown at me, accusations, and then the topper, the threat of court. He actually told me he would take me to court. Again. Take me to court, over Lizzie's surgery.

Now, the old me, that person would have heard the word "court" and immediately begin to feel instant fear, panic, anxiety, get emotional, you name it. The new me was not afraid. For once, I had no fear. I cannot tell you how empowered I felt at that moment. All those years of living in fear that my children would be taken away, it was all gone. Thank God. God was helping me, and I knew it. He was giving me such strength and peace!

Gratitude, beyond gratitude.

The phone call ended and I was calm, and at peace. This was amazing to me. I couldn't believe it. I was not emotional or afraid, not one bit. I simply called my mom, told her what was happening, and asked that she call my brother, the one who was friends with Ron. I wanted him to call and tell Ron not to drag us into court, over Lizzie's surgery. My brother called him, and Ron backed down on his threat.

I knew my job was to protect Lizzie, be the "mamma bear" I was intended to be, plain and simple. Lizzie was still in recovery, and was not comfortable with the thought of sleeping anywhere else but home.

The next morning, I calmly called Lizzie's doctor, and asked about the call Ron said he had made. They had no record of any call, and didn't have any messages from him. It was as I had suspected. Enough. That was it.

2 Timothy 1:7 "For God gave us a spirit not of fear but of power and love and self-control."

I didn't fear, and I felt the power, but I did not feel love, and I wasn't completely in control. I did say a curse word, I believe. But, since I'm new at this, and fresh out of the gate, I wasn't going to beat myself up over it. I simply asked God to forgive me for that part, and thanked Him for the rest.

What a wonderful feeling, to know that this incident, which normally would have caused me to go into over-reaction mode, was just a little hiccup. This enormous change was the obvious work of an awesome God.

I had turned everything over to him, and look at the way things were going now, so very well. He had changed so much in me, I wish this had happened long ago, but I was very grateful it was happening now!

Deuteronomy 31:6 "Be strong and of good courage, do not fear nor be afraid of them; for the Lord your God, He is the one who goes with you. He will not leave you nor forsake you."

I literally felt I could do anything at this point, that anything was possible. I don't remember a single day when I actually felt this strong, this calm, in any situation. I had been transformed so drastically, so quickly, it was unbelievable.

A few weeks later, Ron, his wife, and Hannah came to get Lizzie for lunch. When they brought her back home, the back door to Ron's van opened up so Lizzie could get out, and I could see Hannah sitting there. I calmly said

"Hi Hannah." That was all. She turned to look at me, but did not say anything. She looked surprised. At that moment, the fear I had always experienced before was gone. Fear of rejection, the rejection I had to endure from my own child for years, was completely gone! Even though Hannah could not acknowledge me, the peace I felt in that tiny moment was incredible. The strength that God was giving me was undeniable.

It was a monumental day. A day I had needed for so long. I was so grateful to God for giving this small, but precious moment to me. It might sound insignificant to you, but these moments of strength, courage, peace, are truly indescribable when you've lived in paralyzing fear, and anguish for a long time. This could only be from God, no question in my mind. All of my own efforts had failed miserably for years, God had now taken over and look at the result. It was truly like magic.

The way I thought of God before was completely wrong. I used to think of Him as powerful, but that there was no way He could know every little thing, about everyone, know who we all were, even. I thought He only saw the big picture, and that people like me were actually insignificant. I knew there were ways he could reach people, like a few times he had reached me, but on a day to day basis, and to be this close, it never entered my mind. I could not have been more wrong!

I was never an atheist, but I know plenty of them. I've listened to them talk about God over the years, and it never seemed right, because I had felt something supernatural so many times in my life. I have always wanted to believe completely.

It was always a struggle, always difficult to fully believe, because of all of the influences in my adolescence, and I needed a little proof. When I started watching certain movies and television shows about the "other side," I began to see what I believed was proof of the after life. I had begun to relate things to God, the little "signs," but still didn't have any closeness, and no real understanding. The movies, like the ones pertaining to real stories of people visiting Heaven, those stories nudged me a little inch closer. Chris taking me to the first church I ever felt comfortable in, pushed me a little further.

I was getting there, very slowly, but once I started to plummet into the dark abyss recently, when my life caved in, I know now that God used that time to really reach me. He cleared my life of any distractions, had me so broken and completely alone, to get my attention. I am so thankful He did this for me. I've said it before, that night on my patio, as difficult as it was, truly was the best day of my life, and I mean that from the bottom of my heart.

Chapter 26

Lizzie and I had now been at home for over two months at this point, while she recovered from her surgery. We really only left the house for our doctor's appointments, and for school, or groceries. We discovered at the last appointment that she had grown almost two inches since surgery day, and she was healing very well. We were both natural "home bodies," so we really didn't mind being confined in our home for this long, and never once suffered from cabin fever. There was plenty to do at home.

I had been doing a "spring cleaning," and decided to clean out the closet. I took almost everything out of the closet to rearrange, and clean it from top to bottom. As I was pulling some shoe boxes out, I noticed Chris had left a shoe behind, most likely in his rush to leave. That thought stung a little bit, the idea of him "rushing" to leave us. I was sitting on the floor, holding the shoe. It was a brown colored, slip-on Croc we had bought when he had hurt his foot. It was the "right" shoe.

I had to laugh, through a few tears. Cinderella. In reverse. Not exactly a glass slipper, how unfair that I get an ugly, brown, rubber Croc. We're not fancy people, but, seriously? God does have a sense of humor.

My mind immediately went searching for the meaning of the shoe, wondering if this was a sign, or did he leave it subconsciously because he didn't really want to go? I was over-reaching into every possible scenario, the romantic that I am. Maybe the shoe itself represented our relationship, ugly, brown, and plastic, and I was delusional. My mind covered every aspect of this symbolism, not just the romantic side.

I decided to text him, since we had communicated a little bit, and I asked him if he wanted his shoe. No answer. The suspense grew. Maybe our love story isn't over yet or maybe it is. I would have to trust God and wait and see.

He sent a text message to me later that day, but never mentioned the shoe. We had a bit of friendly conversation. I was happy with just knowing he was still communicating with me. I was content, and thanked God, I knew he was working.

I couldn't help but constantly think about what had happened to us, but more importantly, I thought about everything I had learned recently about love, real love, real unconditional love. I thought about trust, and my inability to trust anyone, especially someone I was in a relationship with. I wasn't sure I could ever trust Chris. I also realized that I had treated him like the enemy for so long, because of everything that had happened in all of my previous relationships.

Looking back, I can't believe we lasted as long as we did! We had many, many good times, and I knew there was love there, but honestly, we did not stand a chance. There were far too many sets of baggage between us, and I know for myself, I had never healed from anything in my past. I knew we were brought together for a reason, and maybe that reason hadn't come to light yet, or maybe he was only supposed to get me here, to the place I am now. Maybe that was his purpose, to get me closer to God. I was grateful for him, and I was grateful I had a new awareness.

More importantly, I knew God's plan was best, and even if Chris was not going to be part of my life anymore, I would be fine. I felt like I needed to help Chris, like he had helped me, get back to God.

I bumped into him briefly, one day, and was shocked at his appearance. He had lost a lot of weight, and looked very different. He didn't look happy and healthy, the way I had envisioned him looking in his new bachelor life. A few days later, Lizzie and I saw him again at the grocery store. Lizzie also expressed shock over his appearance. It was sad, we thought, in just a couple of months, how much he had changed. I knew he was in bad shape, and tried everything I could to help him. I sent him uplifting and inspirational messages I had found on Facebook, some of the same ones that had helped me so much.

He would call me really late almost every night, and even though I needed sleep, I would talk to him, sometimes for hours. I tried as hard as I could to help him. I think I tried too hard. He had once tried to help me out of my darkness, and I fought him at every turn. The tables had now turned, and he was fighting all of my efforts. He was living with so much negativity, so much darkness, and was so stubborn, our communication soon ended, again.

I had gotten my hopes up too much, and felt the pain and heart-break all over again. I began to question everything, going over our entire relationship, all the bad times, all the good. Nothing made sense anymore, and I was beginning to think I didn't even know who Chris really was. He was acting so bizarre, out of character, and the person I had loved seemed dead and gone, and possibly had never even existed. Nothing was adding up.

It was getting easier now to remind myself to trust

God, God's plan. Every time I would slip back into trying to figure it all out, I would quickly stop and redirect my thoughts to trusting God.

I had spent my whole life trying to find my love story, trained and disciplined from childhood to long for that perfect love. Somehow, at fifty, after many failed attempts, I still had a little hope. I am a romantic at heart, and always have been. I can cry over any common romantic comedy, and have a longing for that "moment" of my very own. That moment when you find your true love, real love, the love that would last.

I don't think I have ever been comfortable with the idea of being alone, until now, only after God stepped in and changed my perspective. Growing up with parents that had been together since they were so young, seeing their marriage last until my dad passed away, was something I wanted to do in my own life. I had tried, but had failed, twice. I thought that was what we were supposed to do, and if we didn't, then there was something wrong. This way of thinking forced me to jump into relationships too fast, with the wrong people.

After losing Hannah, I didn't just jump into bad relationships, I think I forced them. I wanted so badly to get the family life I had before, but with someone else, whether they wanted it or not! It wasn't a conscious thing, but it was real behavior on my part. This realization was tough to accept, but God was showing me now all of my choices, mistakes, and as much as it hurt, I was grateful. I felt convicted but not shamed, not condemned. I have not taken criticism well in my life, from other people, but somehow coming from God, it doesn't hurt as much. It's actually a good thing, and can only make you a better person.

Family life is where I felt secure. I don't know if

being adopted factors into this, but my fear of being alone was always very real, even if I didn't realize what I was doing. If I was on my own, I couldn't really enjoy life at all, I could not focus on what I wanted to do, things that would make me happy. All I ever knew in my younger days, was that I wanted to be married, and most importantly, be a mother, this is where I felt most "normal." My entire identity was born from marriage and motherhood. I think of myself before marriage as a lost soul, no identity, with absolutely no worth. Looking back now, I could have had an identity based on all kinds of good things, positive things. God had already blessed me with certain abilities to strengthen my identity, but I couldn't believe any of it because I felt worthless. I needed another person to validate my worth.

I think the disappointment of my first marriage was the reason I married too quickly the second time. Frankly, I had no business even getting into the first marriage. I had no idea what love, or marriage really meant. I'm never going to say I regret either marriage, because I would not have any of my precious children, but I can forgive my mistakes now, knowing I didn't have the knowledge I had needed at the time.

I felt like I was always trying to "make" something from nothing. I was starting to realize that if you start with something great, with God in the center of your relationship, it could be fantastic. Who doesn't want fantastic? Who doesn't want real love?

As down as I was, as heartbroken, as broken as I was over losing Hannah, Lizzie's surgery, and Chris leaving, I would never have this new perspective, and would never have been able to grow. I'm convinced God used my desperate situation, a time when I was completely hopeless, broken, to literally change my entire perspective, and my whole life. He's changing everything about me, the way I feel, act, think, everything. It feels a little like going off to boot camp, I've had so many things stripped away, things that gave me security (I thought), things and people I was dependent on in life to help me through, that were actually keeping me stuck. God ripped the negativity out of my life. There is no other explanation of the changes, but that it's God.

The contentment I felt now, knowing God was working, I could relax and let Him work in my life even if I was alone. There is no possible way I could have ever made it here, unafraid to be on my own, without His intervention.

This would be my time now, time to find my independence. I didn't have a clue what being independent really meant. I knew the meaning, of course, but never understood how to get there, or what I was lacking. I always felt like I had to have someone in my life. I never felt "whole" unless I was in a relationship, and for the first time I wasn't afraid, and wanted to be completely whole before I ever entered into another relationship. Simple. With Chris, I never felt like we were supposed to get married, even though he asked me to marry him four times and I always said "Yes." I was terrified of marriage at this point, and knew deep down he wasn't "the one," but I thought I had to have him in my life. It wasn't even a conscious thing, but I always felt more comfortable having him there, I thought, even if the relationship wasn't healthy or strong enough to survive. My fear of loss overpowered any common sense about the relationship. I could not handle even the mere thought of loss, no matter who it was.

I thought being in a relationship provided comfort, love, peace of mind, security, a partner, someone to be there when you needed strength, courage, and support, and you give the same back to the other person.

My relationships before, including my two marriages, were now looking so shallow, and probably explains my efforts to make something out of nothing. Chris was the first person to really bring me a few steps closer to God. I will always be grateful to him. I could never trust him, or anyone else, really, but I was so grateful for the wonderful thing he had done for me.

I wish we had been better, but to tell you the truth, the way we were, it would have always been a struggle. All of my relationships were a struggle. I'm not talking about working on the things that needed work, like in everyone's relationship, but real struggle. Do you ever feel like you are ignoring some pretty big issues in your relationships, because you might someday be able to "fix" them? Are you a "fixer"? I would refuse to believe the worst about someone, because somehow I would be able to fix them.

God is the only one that can fix or change anyone. He proved it to me when he changed me. I would never have let anything anyone said get into my soul, and change one single thing about myself. I am stubborn, and have even been so stubborn for decades, that I have fought the goodness of God, and fought letting Him in. God has a plan, and I want to live His plan, whatever that means. Maybe He has a man in mind for me, maybe not. I've always thought we were supposed to find our soul mate, and I've had a few.

What is a soul mate? I've had four different men tell me I was their soul mate, only to have all four of them betray me in the worst sorts of ways. I was on Facebook again one day, and I noticed a friend pouring her broken heart out for everyone to see. Her words were so familiar to me. Her man, the love of her life, suddenly breaks up with her after over seven years, because he met someone else. Another soul mate, I assumed. It dawned on me at that moment, why do we count on a man to fill this job? This is, after all, our soul, our being, our heart, our spirit, all of everything we have in the world, and we are depending on a man to protect and cherish our *everything*?

Why do we, men and women, keep looking at humans for this most important job? Why not look to God? God is, in fact, our true soul mate. Instead of trying to find a human being, a flawed, unworthy human being, why don't we just understand it's God's place. From now on, I thought, I want a "partner in God," instead of a soul mate, who can only let me down, and disappoint and hurt me at the highest levels. What a relief to not only realize I already have my soul mate, FOREVER, so the pressure's off, but to realize that having a partner in God would be an extra bonus. Someone to actually be on a journey with, a journey with the most awesome ending, eternity. Someone that God wants in your life.

I can't wait to see what happens in my life now that I know God is working. To feel the strength I feel now, the peace, the love, and it can get even better. I feel God has already changed me so much, and I know I still have much more learning and growing to do. I don't think I've ever been more excited, and patient, at the same time. It's all about God's timing, and I trust Him.

The gifts I have received from God could have only come from Him. No medicine, no therapist, no money could have ever given me this feeling of wholeness I feel. My depression was stripped away, a deep depression that I had been living with for years. My heart is still a little broken, but with time, and trusting God, I know it will heal. I truly never imagined I could feel this happy again, ever. Things I would worry about don't even cross my mind anymore. The future is an exciting place, but today feels just as wonderful, and I'm happy here, for the first time, and at fifty years old. I can't believe I had actually reached a point of wanting to "fast-forward" to the end of my life, instead of looking forward to the end! That can only come from God.

Writing my story now, something I know God wants me to do, and is guiding me to do, feels both humiliating and healing. Before now, I would have never exposed myself to such a level of humiliation, but at this time, it seems inadequate compared to what God has done for me. It's the least I can do, if it helps one soul realize what it took me fifty years to realize, it's worth everything. It's worth it even if it only heals me, so I can spend the rest of my life as a better person, and be a blessing to other people instead of being negative, bitter, and angry at the world. I want to enjoy life, and help others. I want to be a blessing to my children. Anything I've learned now I want to pass along to them, so their lives won't be consumed with pain, depression, anxiety, confusion when things get difficult. I want them to know God is there loving them, guiding them, and they have the power inside of them to fight off evil. I want my girls to be those strong people on top of the platform, the people that know God is with them, and they have strength to get through.

That love story I've been searching for all these years, I finally found it. I feel the most love I've ever felt. To be fifty years old, and have such a secure feeling of love, something I've searched and searched for, is truly incredible. I know it's late in life, but the search has been worth it, every hard year, every struggle, every heart-break, to get here. It's only the beginning, just a few months since I was "reborn," another religious word I never dreamed I'd say about myself, but it's true. I cannot even imagine where I'll be a year from now, if I already feel this changed!

I have had some pretty awful things happen, like everyone, and have lived with a very broken heart for a long time. I was crushed and defeated, and almost gave up completely. I can honestly say I am grateful everything happened just as it did. Even the most horrible things, I am grateful for every experience I've had, because without them I wouldn't be exactly where I am right now. I also know that all of the anger I was living with, especially the anger over having Hannah taken, was only hurting me more. I was especially angry that nothing was happening to the person who took her, or to those who went along with it. It would always bother me, how people get away with horrible crimes, hurting innocent people. I could feel my anger boiling inside of me so often, and thoughts of revenge would enter my mind frequently.

I know now that God is all about justice.

Romans 12:19-20 "Do not take revenge, my dear friends, but leave room for God's wrath, for it is written: "It is mine to avenge; I will repay," says the Lord. On the contrary; "If your enemy is hungry, feed him, if he is thirsty, give him something to drink. In doing this, you will heap burning coals on his head."

He will make sure justice is done, and I don't have to worry anymore, He will take care of everything. It's our job to do good work, be a blessing to those we're supposed to help. I honestly feel like God wants me to get this point across. You don't have to wear yourself out, waste your life in misery because of what people, or life has done to you. He will carry out justice in your life. You just have to trust Him. If you're too busy trying to fight all of your battles, trying to take revenge, letting it consume you, you're not focused on His guidance to live out His plan for you. I know His plan for my life has got to be better than what I've been living, because I don't know how to do it right! He's already got me on a better track with writing, it's helping me with so many things in my life, just know and believe it, He knows best.

The shoe. I'm left with a rubber shoe. It could be worse. I have thrown it away, only to take it back out of the trash. Something to hold on to, or maybe a reminder to be more careful of who I let into my life. I will wait and see what happens there. Maybe I'm going to meet Mr. Right, or "Mr. Right with God," but I know no matter what God's plan is, my real love story has already happened. God. God is the most ultimate love story of all, the story that has the most magnificent, beautiful ending, in eternity. All those years of looking for an unfailing love I could trust, that would last forever, I found it, and it was God, all along.

Chapter 27

The test. Here he came again. Chris. There's got to be a test, right? There's always a final exam at the end of the semester, correct? After all of the weirdness, the attempts at helping him, he started calling, yet again. I got sucked in, yet again. That locked door opened up just enough for me to put my foot in, and he was back. We started spending days together, going to lunch, talking, hanging out. It lasted for a few weeks this time. I still felt like there was something he was keeping from me, but we were acting like friends again. He told me he didn't think he wanted to throw the last four, almost five years away. He told me he loved my soul, loved me, loved my children. It sounded sincere. We spent many days and evenings together, and hours on the phone, again.

This time there was something different, and that difference was me. I was a little more guarded, a little more aware of what I was allowing myself to feel. I looked at Chris differently, also, and saw things for what they were, instead of what I wanted them to be. It felt safer this time. I wasn't investing my heart like I always did before, I was only investing my time and trying to figure out what was going on with him, and what would become of us. He was in bad shape, and I truly wanted to help him in any way I could, without it bringing me down.

It did not take long, but soon God began to reveal things, bad things. He was showing me inconsistencies that I had always noticed before, but would allow Chris to talk me out of believing, and I would doubt myself. My own intuition, the guidance of the Holy Spirit, whatever it was, I had always allowed Chris to make me distrust what I was feeling. God was gently revealing things to me now, and I was not going to let these tactics work anymore. God said "No more." God actually kept telling me, "Enough." I had been so stubborn, and maybe a bit disobedient to God, for not listening before. Here it was now, a real test of my faith, already. This journey was happening so quickly, there were so many changes, I wasn't sure if I was even ready for a test. I was nervous about it, but stayed focused, for the most part, because I wanted to do the right thing this time. Letting Chris go was so difficult before, but now I knew the truth about who he was, and it was painful. I had no choice but to let him go.

He had been lying to me, saying all the things he knew I wanted to hear, totally manipulating me. It hurt. Never before had I seen such an ugly side of him, mean, and cruel. It was hard to accept at first, he had always presented himself as spiritual, sweet, sensitive, and soulful, bundled up with a mass of flaws. I thought I was doing the right thing by always focusing on the good in him. Isn't that what we're supposed to do? I certainly wanted people to focus on any good qualities I have, and not my flaws. As horrible as I say I was before, I did try to believe people were good, but I was embarrassingly naive. I trusted too easily when I shouldn't have trusted at all, and didn't trust when I should have. I had it all so backwards.

Was this the real Chris? Or, maybe this was Chris walking hand in hand with Satan. I was trying so hard to figure it all out. I was in a bit of shock. I couldn't believe he could really be all these horrible things and the last four and a half years had been one great performance on his part. Who can do that for such a long period of time?

I was definitely being tested. Tested over everything I had learned up until this point. First I had to come to grips with the truth, the lies, sort through all of the initial pain of even more betrayal. It was not easy, but I kept reminding myself that this was all of God's doing, this was exactly what He wanted me to understand. I had been praying for God to show me the truth, and there it was. It hurt, all over again, but somehow it didn't seem like the end of the world like it would have before.

I was trying to understand why Chris would take the time to come back, spend three months doing nothing but lie, manipulate, and cry, just to torment me. Why? Why would he even bother? Could he possibly get joy from torturing me? What did I do to him? Was this Satan? Was this the devil trying to destroy me again? I could believe Satan was destroying Chris by just looking at him, and watching him in his misery. Here I was trying to finish up the book, study God's Word, get healed and be a better human being, and Chris is tormenting me? This was going to be a tough test.

Before my meltdown, before that night, I can tell you I would have been a mess and probably would not have recovered if this had happened back then. The confusion alone would have destroyed me. Somehow I was approaching the situation with a broader perspective. I was getting angry and emotional, but it wasn't lasting. It would hit me all at once, suddenly, what Chris was doing, lying and manipulating. It was painful. But, I was getting through. That strength, that "thing" I had always seen in people, that knowing they had that everything would be alright, I was actually feeling it now. I couldn't believe it, I finally had it!

It was still in the very early stages, but I had it. If

you take anything away from my story, take this one thing: you truly can do anything through Christ!

This test, I felt, even with all of the pain, was going to result in something good. I knew God wouldn't bring me to this place without turning it into something wonderful, but I might not experience the wonderful for a while. He wouldn't do all these amazing things for me only to abandon me here. Faith. Trust. I was actually trusting.

Going back over the previous four and a half years, my whole relationship with Chris, this man who brought me to God, I realized that was his purpose in my life. To bring me to God. That part was very clear. I know myself, and I can honestly say, it took someone like Chris to do this very important job. It had to be someone that could completely devastate me. He did this job, and fulfilled his purpose very well. Not only did it have to be someone that could devastate me, but it had to be someone I could truly forgive. Strange, isn't it?

It hit me so quickly, that understanding suddenly of what had happened. I had loved Chris like I was supposed to, as close to unconditionally as I possibly could. I had never in my life, ever loved a man like this. There was something about him that allowed me to love him almost like I love my children, my parents, that close to perfect love, that we all need. I don't know why, or if he ever even deserved it, but for some reason I loved him in this way. I don't even know if he ever really loved me, and it doesn't really matter, because it's not about him, this was about me and what God wanted me to learn.

God loves us unconditionally, God forgives us our sins. We are supposed to forgive and love like God loves us. I had always ended relationships over betrayals, stopped talking to people because they hurt me, so many times. Family, friends, boyfriends, husbands, all of the relationships that had caused me such great pain. I always made the declaration that if someone cheated on me, that would be the end, no question.

When some relationships experience the worst kinds of betrayals, it might be the devil doing all the dirty work, I knew this now. I read something about how Satan attacks relationships that could possibly bring more people to God. That's his goal, wouldn't you agree? Any relationship, whether it's parent and child, a friendship, a marriage, that could possibly bring more people to God, those relationships are especially targeted.

This test I was going through now with Chris, meant that God didn't think I was totally forgiving like I thought I was. It was a little extra widening of my perspective, and I only felt peace when I realized it. There wasn't anything I couldn't forgive, anything. Humans are humans. I was finally truly accepting that a sin was a sin, and all people sin. Sounds so simple, I know, but I still had all these boundaries with my forgiveness, and God was kindly pointing this out to me. I had thought I was already there, but God, of course, knew differently. I was loving God more and more. I was finally getting it, the whole relationship, Father and child. It felt like being parented by the ultimate parent.

I was at a point where I really wanted to dive in with everything I had, and never look back. I could never go back, now, not after actually feeling and living these loving acts from God. I wasn't worried about what other people were going to think of me anymore, that fear was just gone. I hope you can get to that point, as well, it's one of the greatest feelings you can ever have!

I was having to really reach and forgive Chris, this person who had truly ripped my heart apart, deceived me, betrayed me on every level. This person that I really never trusted, strangely enough, but had given him my whole heart. It wasn't as hard as I had thought it would be. As much as he had hurt me, he had also done the greatest, most special thing anyone could have ever done for me, brought me right to God.

I was still struggling with the lack of remorse Chris was showing. I wanted him to admit everything, and tell the truth. He would only say that "God knows, I don't need to admit anything to anyone." It was cold. I wanted him to apologize, sincerely. He had already cried and cried over abandoning Lizzie, and hurting her, but he couldn't bring himself to apologize to me, not really. It was very strange. I thought he would actually benefit from admitting what he had done, and would ask for forgiveness, and we could both move on with our lives.

I was forgiving him, doing my best, to forgive all of it, even if I would never get the apology I wanted. It was difficult, but I had to let it go.

It was so clear. I was finally, once and for all, finally letting go. Finally forgiving completely, not just forgiving on the surface, and forgiving what I always thought was truly unforgivable. Finally understanding, how God wants us to be. Understanding that God couldn't work on me, or my life, if I didn't let all of it go. He would make something good out of my pain, make something good out of this hard lesson.

How in the world could God love me this much? I had been so angry, so depressed, so bitter, and had closed myself off to the world around me. Look what He's done!

I felt like I at least graduated up a little, even if I was still on the baby steps of being a Christian, it was okay, and it felt like great progress. I prayed to God, asking Him to remove any other people from my life that were harmful, now that I could see how He had been trying to do this, while I fought against Him. I realized how many times I had been banging on those closed doors, and was so grateful to understand it now. I prayed that He put only good people in my life, people that were supposed to be there.

About this time, when things were finally calming down, I received a call from an old friend, Grace. I had known Grace since the second grade, and had kept in touch with her over the years. Since Lizzie and I had moved to Austin, I had spoken to Grace only once, and knew she lived nearby. I thought of her often, but since I was still pretty much secluded from everyone, I never really reached out to her. She had heard about Lizzie's surgery, which had now been over four months before, and she was curious about what had happened. We spoke on the phone for a while, and caught up a bit. A couple of days later she invited Lizzie and me out to dinner with her and her family, to celebrate her birthday.

We arrived at her house a bit early, and she gave us a quick tour of their large, beautiful home, over-looking the hills. Grace's dad was there, and pulled up a chair at the piano and listened while I tried to play a couple of piece's with my still partially numb hand. I couldn't resist, it was a beautiful grand piano, the exact piano I dreamed of owning some day. Since my movers had dropped my piano during our last move, some of the keys didn't play most of the time. To have this beautiful grand piano in front of me, I could not pass up a chance to play! I could have sat there all night, it felt incredible. Grace's dad was a great audience, clapping and cheering.

Grace's children were Lizzie's age, and she was having fun, as well, getting to know them. She disappeared into another part of the house with them until we left for dinner. It was feeling so nice to be around Grace, and her family. I felt a little like my old self, my really old self, from years before. It felt comfortable, being with old friends, something I had really struggled with for the last few years.

We arrived at their golf club, set in their beautiful neighborhood, surrounded by gorgeous scenery all around. During dinner Grace's husband left our table to join a table of men, some friends of theirs whose wives were all on a trip together. The kids were all walking around, doing different things around the club. It was just Grace and I at the table, for most of the evening. We were talking non-stop, catching up, filling in the gaps from when we hadn't spoken at all. It was nice, and especially getting to spend time with someone I'd known for most of my life.

At one point we were talking about Lizzie's surgery, and I confessed what had happened with Chris, something I didn't tell many people. I told her God had literally picked me up and saved me.

She began to share an experience with me, and it was comforting to know we were on the same page in life, and the same page about God. Suddenly, she tells me she wants me in her life, especially since we live so close to each other.

It felt wonderful, I had recently been asking God to bring good people to me, only people that were supposed to be in my life, and here Grace was saying these sweet things to me. It was confirmation. I was now seeing so many results from my prayers, and believing without any doubts at all. I needed this so deeply, to have it given to me so quickly was simply amazing.

I felt like my life had become a clean slate, and it was only being filled with good, positive things and people now. Literally a whole new life. Everything seemed new, and I had peace to enjoy the goodness. I was so grateful. How in the world could God love me this much? I kept asking that question, over and over. How could this be possible? I had begun this journey thinking I was the most horrible person in God's eyes. How could He do all these wonderful things for a person like me? He has totally transformed my world, and put me on a good path, the path He has for me. How?

Because that's who God is. That's how He loves us, that's what He wants for us. He is there for you, and He has a path for you, and all He asks for in return is your faith, and to be good to others. He wants you to believe in Him, believe His words, and live out His plan for you, a plan of goodness, because God is all goodness. Take it from someone who fought against it, for almost their entire life, His way is the best way.

So much gratitude.

Yes. Just Yes.

Chapter 28

If you had told me five months ago that you had "felt God," and you had been "reborn," I would have smiled, half-believed you, and said something like "How wonderful." On the inside I might have been questioning your sanity, maybe even your honesty, while at the same time wanting to experience exactly what you were telling me. If you had thrown in a "Hallelujah, Jesus loves you, and Praise the Lord," you would have had me squirming a little, but I would have been a little jealous of your confidence, and your faith.

Sitting on a fence is not a fun way to live. When you are sitting on a fence, sometimes it can feel as if you are living in a perpetual state of confusion. I felt mentally paralyzed, not able to choose one side and commit. I lived there for a long, long time.

Five months ago I was broken, brokenhearted, depressed, lost, angry, bitter, filled with guilt and shame. Five months ago I was consumed with fear, and grief. My emotions were raw and uncontrollable. I was literally going through the motions of life, trying to act as normal as possible. Inside was an inferno, and the fire was beginning to seep through to the outside, for my circumstances were wearing down my walls and they were crumbling. My entire life was breaking apart, along with my mind, body and soul. It was the end, I thought.

The end. I can't believe I thought it was the end. I *knew* it was the end, felt it was the end.

Today if you told me you felt God, and you had been reborn, it would be an entirely different scenario. First, I would smile, probably want to hug you, and suggest we make a pot of coffee to sip while you tell me the whole story of your experience. I'd want to hear every detail. I'd want to know everything. I'd most likely get chills and a few tears in my eyes, because I actually know exactly what it feels like to feel God. I love knowing this, and love feeling so spiritually connected to other people in this way. I never felt that connection so strong as I do now.

It's not the end of my life. It's only the beginning. A brand new beginning, without all the baggage, without all the weights trying to pull me down. A brand new life without letting the enemy keep me in a paralyzing state of fear, sadness, self-hatred, and constant anxiety.

Thirty-three years of trying to figure out why all of these strange, "psychic" experiences kept happening to me. Thirty-three years of feeling like there was something really wrong with me, and feeling morbid.

A lifetime of feeling worthless, full of shame, and not thinking I was good enough. I didn't think I was good enough for God, and was living in condemnation for every single thing I'd ever done wrong. I felt condemnation even for things other people had done to me.

I had wasted so much of my life looking for signs of proof of God, that I failed to notice all the times He was actually right there with me! Longing to hear from spirits of people I've lost, I was sucked into that whole world, not knowing any better. I've learned that God doesn't send angels to give messages from the dead, or allow spirits to speak to us. I still don't understand it all, and I have so much learning to do, but knowing what I know already, I do know God's not going to change his mind. I'm still completely grateful for my experiences of believing my dad, and aunt were speaking through my friend, because either way, right or wrong, it pushed me closer to God.

Somehow God loved me enough to pick me up and let me truly feel His love. I still can't believe it sometimes. He is retraining me, my thoughts, my behaviors, my influences, everything. I know this because every time I try to do something that He doesn't approve of, I feel it. It's a real feeling. I think I've always had it, but I had no idea what it was. I guess I thought it was only my own conscience, but this feeling is so much stronger now.

I realized through my new experience that God had given me so many gifts in life, wonderful gifts. I could draw, paint, and play the piano when I was very young. Why in the world do we let life beat us down to the point of feeling worthless? It's the enemy! If you've ever felt this way, like I have, look at your gifts, and maybe that can help you see your worth. He gives us all different gifts. I saw a message one day that said "Your talent is God's gift to you, what you do with it is your gift back to God." Wouldn't it be nice to know you could give a gift to God? I mean, He's God!

I had always fought against religion, but my instincts were always leaning towards God. The fact that I had those instincts means something, that there is, in fact, God. Why would anyone's natural instinct be pointing to something unnatural? I've been on this search for truth ever since my experience with Mark, and his tragic death. The truth, I have found, was always there, always with me, and it's been constant. It has never changed. I could never trust people completely, and couldn't even trust my own instincts, which is embarrassing to admit. It is such a relief, such a peaceful thing to know you can trust God completely.

He knows you, knows everything that is going to happen to you already. He knows who needs to be in your life. I think this is one of the most exciting aspects of my new future, because relationships have always been a great source of anxiety for me. I'm praying God will give me discernment, to be able to see who is real and who isn't. I can say with certainty, I'm going to be paying close attention from now on. I might even throw that ugly brown Croc in the garbage, once and for all.

I've always been an emotional person, a sensitive person. I learned fairly early in life that this was viewed as a negative thing. Emotional people are unstable people, right? Not necessarily. I am thankful for every sensitive nerve, every emotion I have. Life knocks us off that platform a few too many times and we can turn cold, and our hearts can become hardened. God has melted all the cold away from my heart, almost the instant I felt him take the anxiety and anger away. It will make you look at people so differently, and give you an amazing peace.

Peace. A peace I've never known. No more fear, and I was terrified of everything! Paranoid, scared, so afraid something terrible was going to happen that I could never really enjoy anything good that was actually happening. Do you live this way? I have been scared of death for over thirty years. I'm still here. Even if I go tomorrow, I wasted thirty years being afraid of death. Ridiculous. God has changed everything.

I was always so afraid of being judged, even when I first began to write my story, I still had thoughts of my family judging me for writing about God. Why? They have their own journey, and it's between them and God. I was placed in my family through adoption, for a reason, and whatever God's plan is for me, that was part of it.

The fear of being judged over having a child taken

from me has always been one of my biggest obstacles. All I ever wanted to be was a mother, and when she was taken, I felt like a complete failure. Even though I had two other children, two other wonderful daughters still with me. I still couldn't accept that there could be one person out there that might question the situation, question me as a mother. It shattered me and I let it get the best of me, and shifted every ounce of blame and shame to myself, and believed God was angry at me. No more.

God has shown me nothing but love, and has revealed the truth to me. My heart has healed so much because of this revelation. I am grateful beyond words.

I feel like I'm even getting my sense of humor back, something I treasure. I'm not trying to boast here, but I have always been told I am witty, and fairly funny. I've been responsible for a few people choking on, or spitting out their drinks over something funny I might have said. I have always been proud of this. I have always found joy in making other people laugh. Sadly, I had lost this over the last several years, lost my sense of humor. We need laughter, just as much as we need love. I'm not as funny as I once was, but maybe God will restore that gift, as well. He seems to have "rebooted" everything else about me, so I do have hope.

It has been the most amazing experience I could ever imagine, but things aren't and will never be perfect. There have been some difficult days, especially the days Chris would come back and torture me, and lead me on. The days I wrote anything about Hannah, were particularly tough. The difference now, is that I was getting through these days without it destroying me for long periods of time.

The best way to describe what God has done for me in this respect is to relate it to earthquakes. Our lives are filled with destructive forces, some large, some small. When the "big one," the big 8.0 earthquake hit my life recently, there was total destruction. I didn't have hope, faith, I didn't know I could have God so close to me. When I cried out to Him, He showed up and began to restore everything. Since then, these bad days I've had, these little "tremors", would cause me to sink a little. Now that God is so close, I know I can get through these days with hope, faith, and peace. I'm not afraid of the tremors, and I don't look at every tremor like it's an 8.0 earthquake, like I had been doing for so long. This is the faith I've never had.

Its been seven years since that day I watched Hannah drive away with her father to live with him in Fort Worth. Seven years of anguish, heart-break, and torment. Seven years since I was erased out of my child's life, and the sisterly bonds of my three children were broken, stolen. Our family has lost several people in that seven years to death, babies have been born, there have been many celebrations and special occasions. Hannah should have been part of each and every moment with our family. She has been robbed of so much love. We have been robbed of sharing each of her own special moments and celebrations.

I still have a daughter I can't see, or speak to. I will never "get over" not being able to see her, but I can get through. I know I'm going to be alright, for the first time in that seven years. I understand now the enemy has been working through people that have caused the most pain, for all of us. I know I can forgive those people now, and maybe the change in me can change our situation. I understand now that holding on to all of the anger, and unforgiveness only keeps you stuck right where you are.

I know my girls will be alright, and we will survive this, with God's love and help. That, alone, is tremendous.

I know God is working on Hannah, and I hope some day we are reunited.

I know to some all of this might sound a little magical, and it feels magical, but I did not swallow any magic pill, didn't drink from any magic fountain, this is simply what has happened. This has been my story, thus far, where I came from and where I am today. I can't tell it any other way, and I believe it's exactly what God wanted me to do. The exception was that I didn't just want to write it, I wanted to scream it!

Maybe you are like me, and have believed in God but not really believed you could be close to God, and have felt supernatural things throughout your life. Maybe you've let other people influence your beliefs, or the behavior of religious people has scared you away from God. Does the language, alone, make you uncomfortable? Maybe you're afraid you've done too many bad things and God won't accept you. Maybe you don't believe in God at all. I completely understand all of it, I've either been there, or have known people who have been right where you are.

I realize that as bad as I've had it in my life, the biggest hurts and trials, there are plenty of people out there that are suffering much worse. I don't really remember a time that I was ever angry at God, but I have met people that are angry at Him for letting these terrible things happen to them. Maybe you feel that way, and you never knew how real the devil is, the enemy. I never dreamed the devil was real, and capable of working through people to destroy us, steal our happiness, and cause real pain. Knowing this can change our entire perspective, and only lead us back to healing, joy, faith, and living a good life!

I had something to share and give back to God and

others, but didn't know I had any value. I heard Joyce Meyer that first night say "God loves you." I didn't believe her, at first, because I felt like I was too awful for God to love. I knew she must be talking to other people, because I was not good enough for God.

I quickly began to understand shortly afterwards, that He truly does love us, and unconditionally. I love my children unconditionally, and I will always love them, and be there for them no matter what they do. Understanding this is how God loves us, but even magnified, and He's the most awesome parent you could ever dream of, it makes life seem so much better. After all the love he's shown to me, I am telling you myself that God truly does love you! If I can help even one person believe this, then I know I'm doing something good for God, after He has done so much for me. I'm willing to bear my soul, my life, my failures, because I know in my heart this is what I was called to do.

I'm certainly not an expert on God, the Bible, or any aspect of religion and I'm not going to ever try to convince anyone, or persuade anyone to believe in God. Nobody ever said anything to me that could have changed me, my beliefs, or my life this drastically.

I also want to tell you that there was never a day that I thought, "I'm at the lowest point of my life, I'm considering giving up, and I think I'll write about it, and tell the entire world how miserable and embarrassing my life is." Honestly, this isn't something I would have ever considered before. Realistically, this isn't something anyone would do.

I do know where I was in life, and where I am today, and it is truly amazing and miraculous how completely restored I am. I didn't enjoy being lost, miserable, cut off from people. Every day was a struggle. I wanted life to be over. If you are in a place that even remotely resembles anything I've described, then this might all be written for you. God works that way. It's how He has finally gotten through to me, or I wouldn't be so confident in expressing this to anyone. It's that proof, that truth some of us must have to finally commit.

Writing the first few pages of my story, I already felt very uncomfortable writing "I" so much, which is why I think I had always tried to write more of a novel. Now that I'm at the end, I am more than relieved to be finished, for many reasons. The most important reason, personally, is that I can take my focus off of me, and direct it more to other people around me. I cannot wait to spread my wings and see where I land next. (But no more running, and no more moving.) I'm long overdue for an adventure, and I feel such a sense of excitement, for the first time in years and years.

I'm giving this to God, my story, as humiliating as it could be, giving all I have to give at the moment to Him. I know He's been guiding me, and maybe you're the one He's trying to reach! Maybe you're going to look back and see that He's been in *your* life, all along!

Isaiah 40:28-31 "Do you not know? Have you not heard? The Lord is the everlasting God, the Creator of the ends of the earth. He will not grow tired or weary, and his understanding no one can fathom. He gives strength to the weary and increases the power of the weak. Even youths grow tired and weary, and young men stumble and fall; but those who hope in the Lord will renew their strength. They will soar on wings like eagles; they will run and not grow weary, they will walk and not be faint."

Made in the USA
Lexington, KY
07 June 2016